Leading out of Who You Are

The Undefended Leader trilogy by Simon Walker:

Leading out of Who You Are:
Discovering the Secret of Undefended Leadership
(March 2007; ISBN-13: 978-1903689-431)

Leading with Nothing to Lose:
Training in the Exercise of Power
(forthcoming August 2007; ISBN-13: 978-1903689-448)

Leading with Everything to Give:
Disarming the Powers and Authorities
(forthcoming August 2008; ISBN-13: 978-1903689-455)

"One simple and speedy test for evaluating a book is to open it up and to peruse random single pages. If one's attention is held and something worthwhile is learned, no further delay is justified. The book should be read as a whole. For me, Simon Walker's book The Undefended Leader *falls into exactly that category. I suspect many thinking people would feel a similar fascination, for this book is both a provocation and an inspirational release into a further enlightenment."*
Meredith Belbin, Belbin Associates, Cambridge

The Undefended Leader trilogy and The Leadership Community:

The Undefended Leader trilogy developed out of Simon Walker's work with a number of business and social leaders who make up The Leadership Community. The Community is an ongoing association which is supported by a website: www.theleadershipcommunity.org. You can become a free guest member of the community through a simple online registration process. Membership gives you access to all the online activities included in this book. There is more information on The Leadership Community and its resources in the Afterword on p164.

Leading out of Who You Are

Discovering the Secret of
Undefended Leadership

Book 1 of
THE UNDEFENDED LEADER trilogy

Simon Walker

PiQUANT
editions

British Library Cataloguing in Publication Data

Walker, Simon
  Leading out of who you are : discovering the secret of
  undefended leadership. - (The undefended leader trilogy ;
  bk. 1)
  1. Leadership
  I. Title
  303.3'4

Cover design by Philip Miles
Book design by To a Tee Ltd, www.2at.com

*Dedicated to
my wife, Jo, without whom
this book would never have been written*

I am also deeply grateful to all those who have supported me
over the last seven years on the journey on which this book has
taken shape: Jim, Freya, Nick and Jen and Ben and Tobyn, as
well as many other dear friends.

Simon Walker,
Cambridge

Contents

List of Diagrams

The original pen drawings at the beginning of each chapter and elsewhere are all copyright © 2006 by Simon Walker. The following diagrams further illustrate key concepts:

Preface

About an hour's drive from Kingston, the capital of Jamaica, is the old Spanish port of Ocho Rios, which owes its name to the mistaken belief that eight rivers flow into the Caribbean here. The area boasts one of the island's most stunning natural features: Dunn's River Falls, whose crystal-clear waters descend six hundred feet over terraces of smooth rock to join the Caribbean on the white sands below. If you visit the falls, you will be invited to join one of the tourist groups that are taken up to the top by an official guide. As you toil slowly upwards, holding hands in a human chain, you'll be told to pause briefly at set places, where official photographers pop up and video you. You'll be instructed to sit for a few moments in a pool, to be filmed, 'beaming', before being moved on so the other 19 members of your group can go through the same routine. You'll pass by glorious cascades that tempt you to take a shower, glistening plunge pools that beg you to dive in—yet you'll leave them unexplored. You will be within arm's reach of jets of water that would massage your shoulders and neck, yet you'll stay stolidly in your chain, hands locked, and miss your chance. Through palm fronds you will glimpse magnificent views of the peaceful sea, but instead you'll focus on the grinning faces of your official cheerleaders, urging you to whoop and holler at the 'great time' you're having.

And yet no one at the falls will be doing anything different. Not one single person will be out of line, enjoying the spectacle in any other way than this. Like obedient children, you'll all be toeing the line. You'll pass by all these temptations, still linked hand-in-hand, resenting every missed opportunity, every required pose, every restriction placed on you as you climb wearily up the prescribed route until you are led, an hour or so later, out to the top of the falls. You'll arrive there feeling as if, somehow, what should have been the most exhilarating and liberating experience had been turned into an exercise in being led, against your will, where you didn't want to go.

You will probably reflect that it's a great pity that the Jamaican authorities have imposed these rules that prevent people from being free to just enjoy Dunn's falls for themselves. But at that point you may discover something quite unexpected: that there are no rules at the falls. There are no rules telling people to hold hands, or to walk in line; no rules telling people not to dive in the pools or stand under the cascades. In fact, there are no restrictions at all on how you can enjoy your visit. You can have a natural massage, you can take a jacuzzi, for as long as you like—and no one will stop you. You can do all these things; but you don't. You don't because no one else is doing them.

What happens to every visitor at Dunn's falls is what happens to everyone everywhere. People allow themselves to be constrained by imagined rules they have come to believe are real: rules that determine their lives and experiences. It is a kind of leadership that people have come to follow, a kind that invites them to toil away, in a human chain, up the side of a waterfall. It's a kind of leadership that is quite clearly unrewarding—it denies sensation, experience, pleasure. It denies the essential quality of this place, its energy and raw power—indeed, its power to heal. And yet we submit to it.

People submit to poor leadership, to leadership that is clearly wrong, to leadership that everyone can see leads us away from life and health. We submit to leadership that is full of hypocrisy and deceit, leadership that is manipulative and abusive, leadership that sells us a lie of some future utopia, leadership that lacks courage and is really concerned with securing the leader's reputation. We submit to it because we have come to believe in the imaginary rules. We convince ourselves that it must be right, that our senses deceive us: that there must be some hidden danger in the obviously better way. We accept the rule of the group and we fear being exposed as the foolish, idealistic, mistaken person who stepped out from the crowd.

Yet some of us long—and hope—for a different kind of leadership. We still believe that a leader should say what he means and mean what he says. We still believe that a leader should have integrity as well as inspiration. We still believe that a leader should work for an end greater than her own advancement. We still believe that a leader should be willing and able to make sacrifices. We still believe that a leader should be able first to serve rather than be served.

This is a book about leadership, but not the kind that leads people up waterfalls in human chains. It is about an 'undefended' leadership that invites people to break away from the group and jump into the beautiful pools we see around us. It invites us to embrace a kind of difference that is radically free and exhilarating. It offers us a horizon that is wide and blue. It encourages us to raise our gaze from the usual tacky, commercialized version of the world, compromised and exploitative, to which we have allowed ourselves to be subjected, and believe again that another, freer and more honest kind of life can be ours.

Simon Walker
Oxford, 2006

INTRODUCTION

The Beginnings of the Story

As a young adolescent, I remember being equally fascinated and appalled by the figure of Gandhi in Richard Attenborough's film of the same name. Played by Ben Kingsley, the Mahatma's frail body and defenceless demeanour, his beggar's clothing and scant belongings represented perhaps everything I despised as a young, strutting male. I could hardly imagine a figure like that winning many admiring glances from the girls at my school! And what a contrast with the heroic role models I idolized: muscular athletes, who dominated the opposition with their overwhelming physical strength and breathtaking skill. Gandhi simply didn't fit into this economy of power. In these terms, he simply had nothing to offer: he epitomized the weakness I associated with the boys who were always picked last for every team. He was, to be blunt, a physical and social embarrassment, someone who would have been a pariah if he'd been in my class.

This attitude to Gandhi was not, I came to realize, unique to me or my generation. It was typical of many of the British elite of his day, including Winston Churchill, who scoffed and fulminated at his coming to 'parley' on equal terms with the Empire's high commissioner dressed only in a loincloth.

And yet I had to admit that, despite my prejudices, Gandhi was a figure of remarkable influence, not only in his day but in world history. It was this fact that troubled my immature understanding of power and leadership, because I simply couldn't account for it. My confrontation with Gandhi was my first encounter with an extraordinary historical figure who challenged me on this issue. It was certainly not my last.

I had become a Christian at the age of 13, making my own the faith taught to me by my parents. Up to that point, I had associated Christianity with a number of things that came very low on my list of desirables: old age, buildings that were dull, cold and badly lit, ancient language and rites, out-of-date music and the strange feminine attire worn by vicars. However, the decisive moment for me was closer than I thought. It came without warning one evening in February 1985 when 80 or so pupils—a fifth of the whole school—responded to a call from a visiting preacher in chapel. And I was one of them.

Overnight, the Christian Union became the largest society in the school, and so it remained for the rest of my time there. Perhaps, in a way, that was one of its handicaps, at least in helping me to mature. The CU was influential—indeed, powerful—and so, unlike most Christian teenagers, who grow up being ridiculed and marginalized, my experience was that my religion was something with credibility. Indeed, it got you places. Most of the school prefects were Christians, deliberately chosen by the headmaster for their moral lifestyle (and maybe their compliance). Perhaps it isn't difficult to see why my faith failed to challenge the hierarchy of power I was naturally internalizing as a young adolescent male.

Ironically, Jesus himself became an increasingly awkward figure—something I would spend the next decade trying to resolve. He was a man who, at times, chose to use physical force. The depiction of him as 'gentle Jesus, meek and mild' is deeply misleading. I wouldn't have wanted to be a money-changer in the Temple on the day he overturned their stalls. I wouldn't have liked to be one of the religious leaders whose arguments were torn to shreds and their hypocrisy exposed by his wisdom and insight. He used power to quell raging storms, to multiply a few loaves and fish into enough to feed many thousands and to physically overwhelm those who came to arrest him in the garden of Gethsemane.

However, the more I looked at this historical figure, whose disciple I'd chosen to be, the more I was confronted by another truth. That Jesus had not, in accordance with the rules of the hierarchy I had come to understand, chosen to use power to achieve his greatest and most far-reaching victory. He had used weakness. His death on the cross stood as a rebuke to all attempts by the Church to establish God's kingdom through the use of power, whether physical, economic, political or military. There can be no shadow of doubt whatsoever that at the heart of God's purposes to transform the world is the way of vulnerable self-offering. Christians believe that the single most powerful act by any one person in human history was Jesus' death on the cross. Indeed, they regard it as a cosmic event, which brought into being a new order and reconfigured the entire destiny of humankind. But whether it actually was or not is irrelevant to the point I'm making here. What is beyond dispute is the fact that that crucifixion changed human history as no other human act has done.

Jesus' death has inspired literally hundreds of millions of people to follow him. There are tens of thousands of churches named after 'the holy cross'. Each year, the whole Christian world observes as its most sacred day Good Friday, the day Jesus died. The cross is held high on every Christian march and pilgrimage. It is worn by nuns as a sign of a lifelong vow. In Christian countries it is placed at the head of many graves, in the hope of a life beyond the grave to which the death of Jesus is the doorway. The sign of the cross is made countless times every day by believers who acknowledge that their God died for them on it. Jesus' journey to the cross occupies nearly a half of the Gospel accounts of his life; the entire New Testament is one long interpretation of the meaning of his death and resurrection. More books have been written and read about the day of his execution than about any other single day in history.

As I grew into adulthood, I realized that, although I had followed Jesus for nearly a decade, although I was myself in Christian leadership, my understanding of power and leadership was still basically informed not by the life and death of the man I followed but by the values of the playground, the sports field and the market. Jesus' life and death confronted me with a story of power at the centre of which lay an act of weakness and self-emptying. I had to try to grasp the reality that power is not located only in might. I had to begin to revise the terms in which I made sense of what power is and how it can be used. It wasn't that one had to eschew altogether physical strength, or verbal skill, or force of intellectual argument, in favour of frailty and ignorance. Rather, it was that these things in themselves could not be seen as the pinnacle of power. Any account of power could happily accommodate exhibitions of intellectual, political or military strength around its lower slopes, but it would have to place at its summit the exercise of vulnerability and self-emptying.

Indeed, as I looked more closely at human history I saw this pattern repeated over and over again. There were, of course, many examples of what I would conventionally have called 'powerful' men and women who had changed the course of the world. Military leaders such as Alexander and his Macedonians, Julius Caesar and his legions, Genghis Khan and his Mongol hordes, Napoleon and his *Grande Armée* have reshaped the political landscape time and again. Of course, tyrants have devastated that landscape, including in the last hundred years alone Adolf Hitler, Joseph Stalin, Mao Zedong and Pol Pot. However, in all these cases the will of the leader was imposed, by sheer force or some other kind of coercion. Dictatorship is hugely destructive and rarely lasts long. On the other hand, stable political systems, on which civilizations have been built to survive for centuries, arguably have been founded on strategies that decentralize and disseminate power.

Crude, brutal and coercive forms of power and leadership occupy the valleys and foothills of political history, but the higher you go up the mountain, the more you find forms that are democratic, consensual and educative. Power is in general located less in a single individual and more in the collective, the body of followers. The leader himself uses power for different ends: to empower, educate and enable others rather than to dominate and oppress them. Such patterns of power are associated with the more enduring and stable political systems, societies and civilizations. Certainly, without such patterns of power European and North American civilization would never have flourished as it has or reached the heights of human freedom and culture it has attained.

Right at the summit of the mountain there are to be found the few extraordinary individuals whose occupation and application of power is of a different order altogether. These are what I call the 'undefended leaders'. These are the ones whose life and philosophy have involved deliberate acts of weakness and courageous self-sacrifice. Up here, we find the likes of Dietrich Bonhoeffer, Martin Luther King, Desmond Tutu, Mother Teresa of Calcutta, Nelson Mandela, Mikhail Gorbachev, Aung San Suu Kyi—and, of course, Mahatma Gandhi and Jesus of Nazareth. It is on these pinnacles that the highest ideals and myths of humankind have come to be staked. It is also these undefended leaders who are associated with the greatest revolutions, in which the lower forms of power are overthrown and a bright light is shone upon the truest nature of humanity.

It is in undefended leaders that we glimpse our true potential, and in undefended structures of power that people are set most truly free.

Study questions

1. Who are your leadership role models?
2. What is it about them that you admire and try to emulate?
3. How do they exercise power?
4. Write down five words that describe your own approach to leadership.
5. How would someone else know that you had these convictions from the way you lead?

⮑ On the website, www.theleadershipcommunity.org, join the online forum discussion on 'Your greatest leaders'. You will need to register as a guest member in order to join the discussion. That is a free registration.

ONE

What Makes an Undefended Leader?

HIGH PEAKS ᴏꜰ LEADERSHIP

What exactly makes an undefended leader? Is there something that these great ones, who occupy the peaks, have in common? To identify what it is, we need to consider the particular nature of the task of leadership. Many roles in life can be adequately fulfilled by acquiring the necessary skills. With sufficient training, you can draft architectural drawings, legal documents and financial agreements, for example. But leadership is different. Leadership is about who you are, not what you know or what skills you have. Why is this? There are two reasons: leadership is about trust and it is about power.

A leader leads people from where they currently are to another place, which at first is unknown to them and can only be imagined. To get there, they have to leave the safety and familiarity of their present situation, to embrace an unknown, and perhaps dangerous, future. The task of the leader is to make that change possible—and not only possible but actual. He achieves this by acting as a guide between the known and the unknown. The people don't know the future they are being invited to venture into, but they do know the leader. The leader represents safety and security. People follow him because they trust him. The diagram below illustrates the dynamics of power that exist in any such relationship.

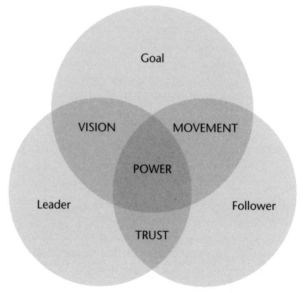

Diagram 1.1   Leader, follower and goal

In any leadership situation, there is a relationship between the leader and the goal. Without a goal, a point toward which people are being directed, it is hard to say that leadership is taking place. The leader's ability to articulate the goal is *vision*; but the relationship between the followers and the goal is *movement*. In other words, the followers have actually to move towards the goal envisioned by the leader. There must be some kind of strategy and tactics to enable this movement to take place—otherwise it will disintegrate into chaos. Finally, a healthy leader-follower dynamic is characterized by the experience of *trust* between them. This is the glue that bonds them together. This is the means by which the followers enter into the leader's own sense of confidence, vision and purpose. The followers appropriate the life the leader is living, and in this way the leader becomes a vehicle for the followers to move into the unknown. This is an appropriate exercise of *power*. If trust breaks down, the connection is broken. Then, either the followers no longer follow or the leader finds other means to ensure that they do—through coercion, manipulation or the like—and so begins to exercise power inappropriately.

When George W Bush was inaugurated as the 19th Republican president of America on 20 January 2001, he could not have known that the events that would catapult him into world history were just unfolding. Some nine months later, on 11 September, when two hijacked passenger planes were flown into the twin towers of the World Trade Center, the tectonic plates of global politics shifted. In the uproar of doubt, fear, grief and rage that followed, the world watched as America struggled to come to terms with an extraordinary and novel experience of vulnerability. Unlike the nation states of Europe and most of the rest of the world, its national security had rarely been breached. Unprecedented security measures were introduced at airports and railway stations across the country. What we were witnessing was a nation attempting to recover a sense of safety that had been shattered. In such times, people look for leadership to make them feel secure. They look for someone they can trust who will comfort them. For America at that time, Bush's simple, black-and-white rhetoric and the political ideology of his neo-conservative allies offered clarity and reassurance amidst the confusion.

Inevitably, the Bush administration has not been able to sustain the extraordinary quality and quantity of trust it at first enjoyed. Critics point to its dogged unilateralism as the cause of this decline, as well as the growing sense of scandal over illegal imprisonment and torture. Some people feel a sense of betrayal, and this feeling is all the more acute because the trust was formerly so strong. This sense of betrayal, as well as confusion, is still growing in America. For the leader, trust is everything: without it, leadership may begin to resort to unhealthy strategies to ensure that people follow. Jim Wallis, one of the foremost social activists in America today, talks of the 'moral authority' of the leader. This, he suggests, is what gives a leader her ability to lead—and this, I believe, is what all undefended leaders have acquired in abundance.[1]

Moral authority is different from the kinds of authority bestowed by election, appointment or delegation: it has to do with the kind of life one has lived. Very often it is acquired only through personal struggle and loss. Consider Nelson Mandela, Winston Churchill, Moses. What do these leaders have in common? The answer is that their most significant leadership did not begin until late in their lives, and those lives were characterized by both struggle and loss.

---

[1] Jim Wallis, *Faith Works: Lessons on Spirituality and Social Action* (SPCK, 2002), pp171ff

Mandela's story is well known. The leader of the ANC's military wing was imprisoned by the South African regime on 5 August 1962 and spent 27 years in gaol. Twenty-seven years! This is the length of time it takes for a baby to develop into a full-grown man or woman with a career well established. Twenty-seven years have elapsed since 1979, only six years after the official end to the Vietnam War. Twenty-seven years Mandela spent waiting, wondering, hoping, despairing, living without ever knowing whether he would be released or done away with, whether the cause he believed in so passionately would ever triumph, at least in his lifetime. Not knowing whether his sacrifice would make any difference at all.

Churchill's political career began at the turn of the 20th century, some 40 years before he was to take his defining role on the world stage. During those years, he experienced cycles of success and failure, marginalization, alienation and defeat. He suffered for long periods from the 'black dog' of depression, and grew used to being pilloried in the media for his military mistakes and political vacillations. It was not until the age of 65, the age at which most men in Britain retire, that he was appointed to lead his country against the wicked ideology of Nazism. He wrote: 'All my life has been a preparation for this moment.'

Moses was, according to the Jewish scriptures, the man God appointed to lead his people out of slavery in Egypt. He is regarded by both Jews and Christians as a spiritual and political giant, a man with such great faith that he led a people maybe a million strong, along with all their flocks and herds, for 40 years in the desert and gave them God's laws for healthy and holy living, the Ten Commandments. He was a man charged not only with rescuing his people virtually single-handed from the power of the Pharaoh and his armies but also with nurturing them spiritually and leading them into God's promised land. However, Moses had to wait until he was an elderly man before God gave him the authority to lead. As a young man he had tried to assert leadership by force and personal power. (Raised in the Pharaoh's palace as a member of his household, he had killed an Egyptian who was in charge of some Israelite slaves). But the Israelites had rejected him and in fear he had fled to another country, to live in exile as a shepherd for many long years. By the time God came calling, he was a crushed man. His old confidence in his own power was shattered, and he asked God many times for reassurance and assistance before he was willing to be a leader again. His early rejection and a deep realization of his weakness and inadequacy had changed him and humbled him.

Now, not all great leaders have experienced significant periods of time in the wilderness, but many have. What is it that sets a Gandhi apart from a Bush? A Mother Teresa from a Margaret Thatcher? A Gorbachev from a Vladimir Putin? It is the same factor: they earned their authority through their experience of personal sacrifice and, often, of struggle and loss. In other words, they all went through the fire of personal experience, by which their characters were tested and refined. For all to see, their personal *integrity* was put under scrutiny, their motives were examined, their commitment and dedication were exposed, their moral *courage* was revealed. In those 27 years in a South African gaol, Mandela was accruing moral authority—the right not only to make a stand against the powers of apartheid but also to command the followership of the ANC. Moral authority is connected with having been proved trustworthy, usually through trial and suffering. What made him, and others like him, remarkable leaders was their remarkable character. Their suffering refined them into more human and courageous moral agents, into people with *compassion*. In contrast, suffering makes many more ordinary leaders cruel, hard and manipulative.

Leaders, it seems, are formed, not simply appointed. This process of formation is not one that is merely passive, or merely active: it is both. Circumstances conspire to create an environment, an arena, in which character is put to the test. Here, the combatants do battle with themselves, in active, painful struggle, wrestling with their inner selves. The battle is against their inner demons—of anger, of the thirst for power that can lurk within all of us. The public, political battles are mere re-enactments of the campaign they have fought and won inside themselves. Indeed, their moral courage and conviction, their personal freedom and security, their willingness to embrace personal loss, are available to them only because they have already fought and won the war with themselves. They have nothing to win or lose on the political front that they have not already won or lost on the personal front. They are free, free of the need to dominate, to conquer and oppress, to consume, to acquire—whether it be land or power or reputation—because they are free within themselves.

Power tends to corrupt, and absolute power corrupts absolutely. The inner character of the leader is revealed and written in large letters on the pages of history because unless she has defeated the inner demons, she will never defeat those outside. Her leadership is merely an expression of who she is inside. And that is what gives such leaders their power and their authority: their freedom to be themselves, to be authentic, to choose their own paths.

It is for this reason that the journey we are going to make in this book is a vital one. We need to try to understand the mechanisms by which leaders can become free. There is an urgent need for such leaders in our world today. Think of the scale of the political and economic choices being faced by our national leaders, and of their consequences, even as you read these pages. What are they going to do about nuclear 'rogue' states such as North Korea and, potentially, Iran? Are they going to foster understanding or misunderstanding between the Islamic world and other societies? How are they going to address the root causes of the expected 3–4°C rise in global temperature over the next 50 years? To deal with the predicted two-metre rise in sea-levels over next 50 years, which could destroy millions of human lives? Are they going to allow the development of cloned and genetically screened babies? To sanction euthanasia? Will they do something to prevent the deaths of some 15,000 children a day due to infected water sources (an intervention that would cost a mere $6 billion)?

Such huge issues overshadow even the greatest of those faced by the leaders of past generations. Never before have we been so aware of the interconnectedness of the choices our leaders make. We can appreciate the impact of our social behaviour not just on our town or our county or our nation but on the entire population of the world, and not only now but for centuries to come—and not just the human population but even the other species with which we share this planet. However, notwithstanding this change in scale and complexity, the leaders of the past still set us a standard of the fundamental moral courage required by every generation of social and political leaders. The choice of Abraham Lincoln to take a stand against slavery was not without ramifications, economic and political. The choice of Martin Luther King to persist in resisting segregation non-violently was not without great cost, to him and others. The choice of Franklin D Roosevelt to throw the might of America into the war against Nazism rather than fighting exclusively against Japan was not without risk.

Virtually every significant decision that has proved to be for the good of humankind has come at a cost. It is rare that legislation that liberates slaves, or insists on a basic wage, or releases countries from debt, or creates equitable trade laws, or exposes corporate fraud, or educates the poor, or provides health care for the vulnerable, increases productivity or is otherwise cost-effective in the short term. And that is one of the great problems facing the democratic world today: change for good often costs more in the short term, but our electoral systems make it very difficult for governments to pursue long-term policies. Those who adopt policies that cost in the short term often lose power.

What we are beginning to realize is that not only do we need individual leaders to be free in themselves, we also need our systems to be liberated. Just as individuals find themselves trapped by the dynamics of power, defending their own interests, protecting themselves against various threats, so too do governments. It has always been so, but since the Second World War the structure of democracy has increasingly been influenced by the mechanisms and values not of the community but of the corporation. The dominant influence in politics now is the market, not the members of a society. Governments 'sell their ideas' to the public, who have already been assessed through focus groups to ensure that what is on offer is just what consumers want. People 'buy' policies just as they buy shampoo. In such a feedback system, where there is a rival brand offering an alternative range of goods to attract any dissatisfied customers, it's difficult for anyone in office to propose any radical or costly choices if they want to stay there.

Perhaps the greatest challenge facing the leaders of Western society is not the development of democracy in countries currently governed by other structures of power but the reformation of our own democracy, which now looks more like market economics than a political system. However, I would suggest that such goals cannot be attained unless we first establish the basis on which a person can be genuinely free. Only when individual leaders start to make different choices, embrace different aspirations and develop a different political vision can such grander questions be addressed. How such a social system as ours may be reformed is the subject of the second and third books in this trilogy. This present book considers the mechanisms of power and of 'defendedness' at the level of the individual and asks just how someone can truly become an 'undefended leader'.

Study questions 1

1. Refer to Diagram 1.1 on page 6. Describe a situation in which
   - vision was weak. What was the consequence for the followers?
   - movement was weak. What was the consequence for the followers?
   - trust was weak. What was the consequence for the followers?
2. Contrast these with a situation in which all of these factors were strong. What was the outcome in this case?
3. Complete the following table to measure a leader you admire, a leader you do not admire and yourself by these three criteria: integrity, courage and compassion.

CHARACTERISTIC	A leader you admire (1-10)	A leader you do not admire (1-10)	Yourself (1-10)
INTEGRITY			
COURAGE			
COMPASSION			

4. Reflect on the score you gave yourself. How do you think you can improve in the area you have identified as your weakest characteristic?

5. Choose two of the issues below that you are particularly concerned about:
   · the environment
   · health
   · education
   · the economy
   · national security
   · foreign policy
   · business

What costly decisions do you believe our political leaders need to take with regard to each of those issues? How would you have to change your current lifestyle to support those decisions?

⮑ On the website, www.theleadershipcommunity.org, join in the online forum discussion 'What kind of leaders do we want?' You need to be registered as a free 'guest member' in order to join the discussion.

PART I

HOW LEADERS DEFEND
THEMSELVES

TWO

The Hostile World of the Leader

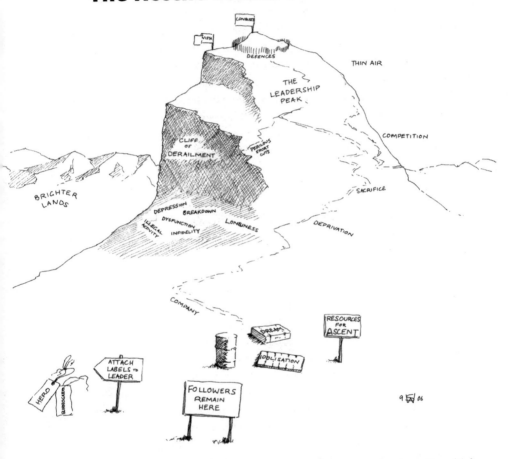

Let's begin at the beginning. We need to establish the mechanisms by which leaders become defended. In order to do so, we must examine the environment in which leadership takes place. This is a particular one, for leaders often experience three things that other people experience only to a lesser degree: idealization, idealism and unmet emotional needs.

Psychologists tell us that what lies behind 'hero worship' is the experience of idealization.[2] Every single person on this planet lives with doubt—confusion, self-doubt or even, for some, self-loathing. Yet few of us are brave enough, or have sufficient support, to deal with these flaws in our own life. So, what do we do with them? We bury them—and then we look for someone else through whom to live a surrogate life. And this person may well be our leader. Many followers need their leaders to be everything they themselves struggle to be: they need to believe in someone who doesn't doubt, who is never defeated, who doesn't fall for the same routine petty temptations that they do. As followers, we need to see someone who is 'other' than us, different and, often, more powerful. We need a superman or superwoman who is strong enough to protect us, to defend us and our way of life against the battering that all of us take. And so we idealize ordinary people who have taken up the burden of leadership and we turn them into the ideal heroes we need them to be.

By doing this, we 'deal' in a way with our deficiencies. We don't deal with them properly or honestly, within ourselves: we deal them through a kind of proxy. The leader lives out our life for us. He embodies all we would hope, but cannot manage, to be. This is at its most basic a strategy to abdicate responsibility—it lets us off the hook and allows us to carry on dallying with the compromises in our lives rather than dealing with them directly. So, a kind of transaction takes place in which we allow the leader to become the person we need him to be. At the same time, the leader, gratified by the attention and, indeed, adulation, seeks to achieve the standards we are unconsciously setting for him. When this occurs, a collusion is established in which both parties meet their needs through the other. This can result in a kind of paralysis. For the followers, it may lead to dependence; for the leader, it may lead to isolation, loneliness and intolerable strain. He cannot share any of the issues he is struggling with inside, because no one will allow him to.

The second experience common to leaders is idealism. Most leaders are to some extent idealists. They have a desire for things to be different, to be better. Thus, the leader lives all the time with a discrepancy between the world that she wants (and wants others) to inhabit and the world she (and others) actually do inhabit. Psychologists call this condition 'cognitive dissonance'—there is a discord between the reality and the ideal. Now, there is plenty of evidence to suggest that this discord produces a certain mental and emotional strain in people. This can be constructive, generating passion, drive and energy; but it can also be destructive, producing frustration, disappointment and confusion. Accordingly, one of the mind's strategies to deal with it is denial and repression.

---

[2] Manfred Kets de Vries, *The Leadership Mystique: A User's Manual for the Human Enterprise* (Financial Times Prentice Hall, 2001)

Most people deal with cognitive dissonance fairly effectively simply by choosing to look away from the ideal. They come to tolerate the reality by avoiding the evidence, by filtering the data they receive. They fabricate a world in which the discrepancy is less.

The leader, however, is motivated by a desire to hold on to the ideal—indeed, it is the ideal that drives her. Accordingly, she commits herself to a journey that will inevitably lead her into a dissonance between the reality and the ideal, a tension that she refuses, until she gives up leading, to deny or suppress. Unfortunately, most other people don't want to know about this tension: they are in the business of denial and they don't want to be reminded of how bad the reality is or how much better the ideal is. They prefer blissful ignorance—and the leader, in all the evangelical fervour of her vision, is a fly in the ointment. And so the leader finds herself pursuing the lonely path that all prophets and visionaries down the ages have followed—of being isolated, being a voice crying in the wilderness, travelling alone, ahead of the crowd, on the margins, in a distant land—feeling a sense of belonging but also a sense of alienation.

The third experience common to leaders is that of unmet emotional needs. Not all of those in positions of leadership are what you might call 'appropriate' leaders. The thing about appropriate leaders is that they take responsibility for people other than themselves. Not all of those who hold positions of leadership do this—and, conversely, not all those who do this are in positions of leadership. But for the purposes of this book I am defining a leader as one who takes responsibility for people other than himself. A mother in the home is a leader; a playgroup facilitator is a leader; a traffic policeman is a leader. Leadership happens when a person takes responsibility for someone other than herself. And leaders do this because, by and large, they care. They care about the welfare of the other person or people. It is not enough for them merely to live a happy, contented life: they are affected by the welfare of others around them. Many leaders respond empathetically to the emotion of the situation around them. To some extent, they 'feel' that situation themselves and experience feelings that are not originally their own. They carry other people's feelings; they are what is called 'empathically open' people. That is why psychopaths are technically the very opposite of leaders: they feel nothing and have no sense of anyone's pain or emotion or welfare but their own. One of the most worrying findings of research in recent years is the number of 'leaders' of corporate organizations who display some psychopathic tendencies. A person who feels little or nothing for another person regards them merely as a commodity or a utility for their own benefit. Other people are merely an extension of their ego, to be coerced to fulfil their agenda.

Appropriate leadership, in contrast, involves being open to the other person's agenda, and genuinely responsive to their needs. Indeed, in many cases the leader, driven by his ideals, sacrifices his own needs for the sake of others. What funds this transaction is another kind of collusion: the leader discovers that by attending to other people's needs, and neglecting his own, he receives approval and appreciation from his followers. This quickly comes to compensate for his own, unmet needs. Thus, a cycle of deprivation and collusion becomes established. The social leader does not meet his own needs directly, but instead meets them through his service to other people, who then reward him with approval. The followers are used to make up the psychological deficit within the leader.

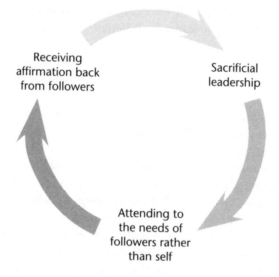

Diagram 2.1   The leadership-followership collusion cycle

The outcome of this is deeply unhealthy. The followers are, to some degree, being exploited by the leader in accordance with his own needs, rather than being led in accordance with theirs. The leadership is compromised because the motives behind it are mixed. Moreover, the leader finds it increasingly hard to manage without this emotional feedback, and so it becomes increasingly difficult for him to share his burden and accept support from others. Instead, he develops an attitude of martyred resignation. He sees himself 'pouring out' his life for the sake of others, while no one cares for him and his needs. This reinforces his sense of identity as the sacrificial one who is specially able to bear the burden of this lonely road. He agrees to travel it because it fits in with a corrupted version of the story of his identity which he continues to tell himself.

Idealization, idealism and unmet emotional needs: a triad of experiences common to those who lead. Together, they contribute to making the environment the leader inhabits an isolated and rarefied one. Leadership is rather like climbing a mountain. The motivation for the climb is the view from the top and the sense of achievement that drives you on through the hardships and privations it involves. From the summit, you will enjoy vistas unseen by others. This is what drives the leader: to find a land currently uninhabited, a better place, a bigger world—be it a happier office, a more effective and higher-performing team, a better-educated school, a more authentic church, a more potent NGO. As you climb, so the air gets a little thinner, and the flora and fauna a little less rich. The surroundings are harsher and offer less protection, and less sustenance. There are fewer travellers along the way, and long periods of isolation in which you walk alone, bearing the weight of the journey in private.

Along the way, you question whether it is really worth it. Why not be content with an easier ride back down in the valley? Were things really that bad that you had to get off your behind and set out on this great quest? Surely you could have waited for someone else to fix the problem? Alone, up on the mountain, the leader is beset with doubt. Her ability to 'self-talk' becomes a vital aid to her survival, because it is in internal conversation that she finds the motivation to continue. Some of these 'mountains' are really only foothills and can be scaled quite quickly; but others are a lifelong challenge requiring fortitude and endurance. It is not uncommon for the toil to take its toll. Many a leader of a big organization is only too conscious of the sacrifice involved in getting where they are: sacrifices they have made in working late, studying longer, putting in the extra mile; sacrifices their family has made, seeing less of Mum or Dad. The leader reckons that now she is there, up at the top, she had better make it worthwhile. She plants her flag and stakes her claim and tries to chase off any rivals. It is difficult for someone who has given up so much not to be possessive about the rewards they finally achieve.

Meredith Belbin, the author of the widely-used instrument Belbin Team Roles, has spent a lifetime investigating how human beings work together. His analysis has led him to the conclusion that for much of history leaders have come from the 'warrior' element in the human species. Belbin identifies the confluence of both genes and cultures that result in the establishment of strong cultural norms, or 'memes'. The further back in history we look, he argues, the more we see the dominance of the warrior meme in shaping the human population.

Of course, every empire has been established by military might, and this has been accompanied by a certain cultural expectation of how you behave when you are victorious. For example, the victor claims the spoils of the vanquished, taking possession of what they have fought over. He acquires goods from his victory as his rightful property. He can rightfully demand the submission of those he has defeated. In many ways, it seems we have retained at least some of these ancient 'warrior' notions in our expectations of leadership. In all too many corporations, the CEO—whether consciously or unconsciously—expects the perquisites of the victor: the vast salary, a rich tribute to the ruling monarch; cultural symbols such as a grand office, a chauffeured car, a corporate jet, which indicate social position and authority; the power to reconstruct the company, probably seeing off the old guard and establishing a new corps of acolytes and ministers. Look at it another way and we begin to see how ubiquitous this notion of the rewards of leadership really is: how many CEOs of major corporations forgo the opportunity to be rewarded in these ways?

The consequence of this is, of course, territorialism. Manfred Kets de Vries suggests that the leader spends his whole time looking for the person who is going to succeed him, so that he can kill them off before they do.[3] There seems to be plenty of evidence that the warrior attitudes of our forebears, whilst expressed today in slightly more sophisticated ways, are still prevalent in our corporations and governments. After all, testosterone—the hormone that makes males territorial and competitive—has not simply been banished by feminism and the emergence of the 'new man'. Indeed, some would argue that many women have had to adopt traditional masculine tactics to succeed in corporate cultures.

If the leader finds herself climbing a mountain, and coping with the privations that involves, she must also deal with the natural hostility of her competitors along the way. There are others just a little lower on the slopes searching hungrily for a short cut, some way to leap into the lead and depose the 'king of the hill'. When they smell blood, just watch them gathering for the kill—they won't waste a minute in seeing off a wounded rival. In the name of corporate effectiveness and share value, there is often little time for compassion in business leadership.

Of course, not all environments are as hostile and as ruthless as this. But I suspect that any of us who have set out on the ascent, be it as the mother of a family, or the governor of a school, or the chair of a multinational, will be aware of the pressures involved in the journey: idealization, idealism, unmet needs, a deprived natural environment creating a sense of loneliness, along with challenge along the way. Perhaps it is no surprise, therefore, that, according to Kets de Vries, 70 per cent of executives suffer some kind of heavy fall at some stage in their career. A recent survey of church leaders in Britain suggested that

---

[3] Ibid., p117

30 per cent had felt like leaving the ministry for a long period of time—and in fact on average 150 church leaders *do* quit every year.[4]

When I was leading a large local church in southern England, I myself suffered from a prolonged bout of depression. At 27, I had found myself in charge of an organization prematurely. However, the root cause of my depression was not circumstantial but personal: I had entered full-time Christian ministry without paying attention to the formation of my own emotional character. Many of the defences I will describe in the coming chapters I have used myself as strategies to cope. Ultimately, it was not my environment that needed addressing, it was me. I am glad to say that I sought help from my local doctor. He was an approachable and sympathetic man who was able to provide me with the appropriate medication to shore up my collapsing ego and clear some space to begin the process of rebuilding—one that would take the next four years. I can remember him looking at me as I described my symptoms on my first visit and saying, 'You would be surprised at the number of clergy I see who are in the same situation as you.'

That experience remains the spur for me to help other leaders, especially those with a social conscience, not merely to survive but to thrive in the task of leadership. It has urged me to try to gain an understanding of the psychological strategies that lead every day to the downfall of leaders. I get the chance to address a group of leaders who are about to set out on the climb—at the start of their career or their ordained ministry. I tell them first that they are all, every man and woman of them, brave people. There are many who do not have the courage to stand up and be counted, many who remain contentedly at the bottom of the mountain, who hope that someone else will fix their problems for them. Whatever they are feeling, however frightened they may be, they are brave and rare people. And then I say that I, for one, am not prepared to stand by and watch as they devote their lives to their mission to make the world a better place and end up limping, battered, bruised and maybe defeated as the reward for their courage. I don't want to reach the age of 65 and look around me only to see the wayside scattered with the broken bodies of those who got lost, or were undone, or simply fell exhausted after they had given their all. It seems to me that anyone noble enough to attempt this journey deserves better than that, and it is our responsibility to assist them.

With these thoughts in mind, let me turn to some of the bad strategies leaders will use along the way from which they will need to be rescued.

---

[4] Statistics taken from 'On the Long Haul' (Arrow Leadership Programme, CPAS), adapted from James Lawrence, *Growing Leaders: Reflections on Leadership, Life and Jesus* (BRF, 2004)

Study questions 2

1. What does it feel like to be idealized?
2. What do you do with your doubts and failings when you are idealized by your followers?
3. What were the ideals you set out with as a leader? Do you still have them?
4. Diagram 2.1 on page 18 suggests a pattern of leader-follower collusion. What are the consequences of this for both?
5. What does it feel like at the top of the mountain?
6. Think of your life as a leader like a journey:
   · What will you pack as you prepare to set out that you'll need to make it to your destination?
   · What breaks will you plan along the way?
   · Will you travel alone or will you find a trusted companion?
   · If you have already embarked on this journey, how do you think you are doing at the moment?
   · Are there any issues you need to address at the moment?
   · How will you know when you have arrived?

⊃ On the website, www.theleadershipcommunity.org, join in the online discussion 'What's your leadership journey?' You need to be registered as a free 'guest member' in order to join the discussion.

THREE

Strategies of Defence I:
Front and Back Stage

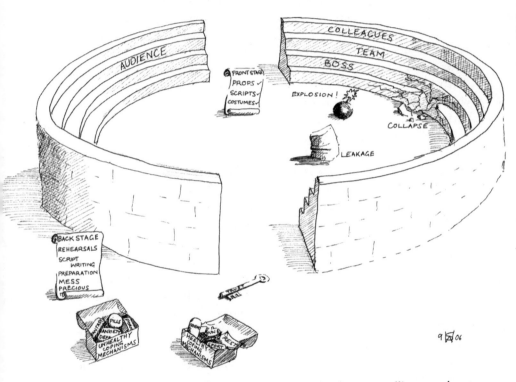

A young former executive, sitting in a chair in our garden, was telling me about his life as the managing director of a successful City consultancy. He described the tremendous stress he experienced in the role, and explained how, in the winter especially, he would often suffer from long periods of apathy, exhaustion and loss of confidence. 'How did you cope?' I asked. 'I would take myself off, snatch a moment when I could escape, and go and sit in the corner of the lobby of the neighbouring office. I could be unseen there, could curl up for a moment, have a nap, and be safe. When I went back into the office, of course, I would have to lead shareholder meetings and sales presentations. You can't stand there and look exhausted—I would have to pick myself up, smile and exude confidence again.'

I guess that everyone in positions of public leadership can identify with that experience. Even if we ourselves have not suffered so acutely, all of us will remember occasions when we have almost literally had to force ourselves out onto the stage and wring a performance out of ourselves, although every fibre of our being was crying out to find a warm, dark corner where we could simply sink out of sight.

Back in the 1960s, the psychologist Erving Goffman based a theory about human behaviour on the metaphor of a theatre. He proposed that, instead of looking inwards at where our behaviour comes from, we should look outwards, at what our behaviour is trying to achieve. Goffman suggested that over time behaviour develops as a strategy to reduce the risks and threats presented by other people. In his terms, the audience we face moment by moment may be either friendly or hostile. Our personal behaviour is a performance intended to ensure that the response is favourable. Each of us develops a routine that we perform every day, and tries to get the attention of the audience we want, who will give us the kind of reception we seek, affirming our sense of identity.

Any leader will immediately resonate with Goffman's idea, because leaders understand the 'need' for a certain amount of self-promotion. Let's imagine, for example, that we know ourselves to be highly intelligent, able to complete mental tasks quickly. We arrive in the office and are assigned a new project by our CEO. We set to work—we can accomplish the task quite easily and swiftly, perhaps more so than the colleagues who are also working on it. In order to please our CEO and secure his approval—not to mention other rewards—we want to do the task well, and we want him to notice this. Thus, we have to succeed on what Goffman calls our 'front stage'. It would be no good if we achieved the goal but kept it so quiet that no else heard about it. If we are really concerned to have our CEO's approval, we will go out of our way to make sure that he sees our success. We will become our own PR agents, publicizing our success on our front stage in subtle but unmissable ways. Thus, we learn to present on our front stage whatever will win approval.

However, suppose we are also anxious not to lose favour with our fellow board-members. We don't want to be seen as self-promoting or arrogant. Really, we want them to see us as skilled but modest, concerned about the welfare of others, not just our own. If this is the case, we will need to use our stage differently. We will still want to do the task well, but we will probably hold back from broadcasting our success. One strategy may be to achieve it but keep it 'backstage'. Then, when our CEO asks how we are all getting on with the task, other people can come out front and shout about how they have achieved it and so on. We will look pleased and applaud them, having cleared the space on our front stage for someone else to shine, not only us.

On our front stage, we ensure that we present and promote the right signs, props, evidence and script to win approval or success or make relationships.

When we do this, our back stage becomes the repository of the ideas, thoughts, relationships and experiences that could undermine our frontstage performance.

Of course, the spotlight will fall on us in due course as the CEO asks us how we have done; and then we will quietly but confidently invite him backstage to see our work. Surprised and pleased, he will be doubly impressed, not only that we have achieved the goal but also that we didn't boast about it but instead allowed others to shine. By keeping things backstage, we appear modest; but we also reduce the risk of being rejected—and if our colleagues fail, we can conveniently distance ourselves from their failure. We can make sure we don't show anyone our deepest desires, needs or achievements until that person has proved trustworthy, and until we have prepared thoroughly to ensure that they are well received. We don't want to risk them being judged and found wanting! Thus, we also learn that sometimes it can be effective to use our back stage.

We may hold back from presenting our success on our front stage and so avoid being thought of as big-headed and self-promoting.

We may hold back our real success and true performance until we trust others enough to let them see them. In that way, we protect ourselves, but also secure a deeper attachment from those we allow backstage.

So, our front stage becomes the place where we perform for our audience—often more than one audience at a time. We find ways to secure approval and praise, perhaps of many different audiences at once. Of course, there are many other strategies we will use front- and backstage. What is important to understand is that all our strategies are to do with self-presentation, or 'impression management'. Impression management is the selective revealing or concealing of our personal story in order to secure the response we need from our audience.

This behaviour is not unique to leaders—we all do it. However, as we have seen, there is a very particular and demanding audience watching the performance of the leader. Unlike that at an ordinary performance, her audience is being invited to believe in—and, indeed, often take part in—the drama that is being enacted before them. Their commitment is much greater, and their needs are much bigger. There is a heady mix of idealization and collusion and surrogacy going on, the usual implicit psychological contracts between the leader and her audience. How, then, does the leader perform in order to live up to the audience's collusive expectations? For one thing, by developing a highly refined script, one that she knows will have the desired effect. For another, by arranging certain props on the stage to reinforce the drama and persuade the audience to believe. For another, by adopting certain roles she has learned to play in order to elicit particular emotional responses from the audience. For another, by putting on different costumes to make each role more convincing. In this way, the leader develops a whole set of frontstage strategies to elicit what she needs from her audience.

But this frontstage performance cannot take place without a back stage in which a whole host of other things are going on. There are many things that the leader learns can't appear on her front stage: the audience wouldn't allow it! They need the leader to act out an idealized life, of course, so where does all the less-than-ideal stuff in her life go on? Out the back. And so the leader's back stage may become the repository for all that she cannot make visible—the doubts, the confusions, the ambiguities and the defeats. The front stage is the place for conviction and confidence, the back stage the place for struggle and uncertainty.

The leader may put on a bravura performance on the front stage, hiding away the messy stuff backstage where he hopes it will not be seen.

Nonetheless, the back stage is not only the place for the messy stuff: it is also the place where the script is written, learnt and rehearsed. Here, new ideas are generated and tried out. Here, the leader works with the material the audience could not cope with—the radical thinking, the new possibilities, the real issues. The leader protects the members of the audience from all of this, because he makes a judgement that they would find it too unsettling. Thus, he selects what he is going to put on his front stage.

The leader may hide themself away in their back stage, finding the front stage threatening. It may be hard for people to see what is really going on.

A leader who hides away his thoughts, dreams, plans, hopes and feelings backstage may suffer by being remote from his followers. He may be frustratingly detached and aloof, concealed behind a public persona that gives away little of the true story. He may himself feel trapped, obscured and misunderstood. Unless he find ways to express himself effectively on his front stage, his strongest gifts may never come to light.

Of course, the reality of the two stages is that the central experience for the leader is of living two lives: a public life frontstage and a private life backstage. The former conforms to all his followers' expectations. It represents all they need it to represent—a model of how to live by this or that set of values. It is, quite literally, a public life, a vicarious life, a surrogate life. And then there is the leader's backstage life, in which he struggles with all his own unmet needs and unresolved problems. This is where all the frustration, the disappointment, the doubt, the failure, the weariness get pushed. This is where the leader puts into effect other, private, sometimes secret, strategies to meet those needs and resolve those problems. If they are healthy strategies, they may include things such as making time for personal retreat, for physical exercise, for emotional support, for converse with friends, for sexual fulfilment with his spouse, for secure, confidential relationships in which he can be honest and real. If they are unhealthy strategies, they may include tax evasion, illicit enterprises for personal gain, infidelity, looking at pornography, lying, stealing, depression, domestic abuse and so on.

Now, what we need to grasp is that the front and the back stage are always connected. In fact, their relationship is reciprocal. What happens on the front stage drives what happens on the back stage, and vice versa. So, for example, when expectations on the front stage are very high, the back stage becomes the necessary place to live out another kind of life, free of that pressure. Reduce the pressure and the need for that backstage life will diminish; raise it, and the need will increase.

Many men masturbate, for example, not because they crave the sexual release but because they feel impotent in other areas of their life. The backstage habit is a direct response to a deficit of power on the front stage. The reverse of this is seen with many young women, whose inability to control their back stage leads to attempts to control their front stage instead. Most adolescent girls who engage in self-harm do so because they are unable to master some deeply rooted anxiety or fear within themselves— a consequence perhaps of sexual abuse, or of a breakdown in family relationships, or of a deep unhappiness about their appearance. While they cannot control whatever is causing their anxiety, they can control some element of their front stage. They can harm themselves, they can starve themselves, they can eat and then make themselves sick; they can become obsessive about some habit or practice. These disorders and neuroses all share the characteristic of displacement: dealing with something else as a substitute for the real issue. Indeed, the displacing activity often offers some kind of neurochemical compensation. So, for example, cutting yourself releases endorphins which generate a powerful sense of being alive. When someone is numb inside, such a stimulant may be the only means they have to recover feeling. In such ways, an unresolvable problem on someone's back stage will often lead to compensating strategies on the front stage.

Thus, our front and back stages work together in our complex psychological make-up to contrive ways that enable us to cope. If there is a problem or deficit on one stage, often the other can offer a compensating or displacing solution. In this way, the mind is allowed an escape route, a way to avoid dealing with the pain and attend to something else. This strategy is present in any leader.

The second thing we need to appreciate is that the more attention we consciously pay to one of our stages, the less we will be able to pay to the other. This is almost self-evident. We know very well from our own experience that if we are focusing fully on one activity, it is difficult to give much of our attention to anything else. The person who devotes themself to their frontstage performance has very little spare attention to give to their backstage life. The same is true the other way round. We see this all the time: the academic who is clearly so absorbed in his private world that he is completely unaware of his shabby appearance and poor social skills, the executive so focused on her status and performance she hardly notices the disintegration of her personal values and relationships. There are now service providers who cater for executives experiencing this kind of disintegration, who organize their laundry, their shopping, their holidays, even buy birthday presents for those they 'love', all because there's no time for a busy frontstage performer to attend to such backstage concerns.

Third, we need to realize that the two stages can never be kept completely separate—what goes on on one stage will always make itself visible in some way or another on the other. One of the ways this happens is through leakage. Very often a leader's backstage life will leak onto their front stage, and this is particularly so when the front stage requires a high degree of emotional discipline and other-person-centredness.

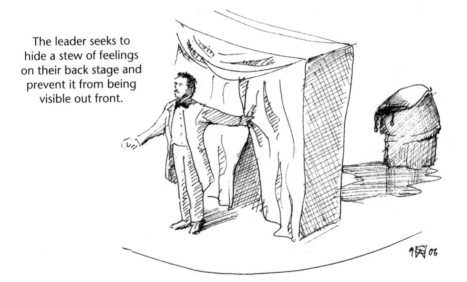

The leader seeks to hide a stew of feelings on their back stage and prevent it from being visible out front.

Social and spiritual leaders and those in caring professions often suffer in this way. Their own unmet emotional needs, pushed backstage, generate resentment, envy, pride, anger or even rage. The pressure of these powerful feelings builds up backstage, until they begin to leak out onto the front stage. People will detect a note of aggression in the leader's tone of voice, an unreasonable irritation when things don't go her way, a certain surliness or mean-spiritedness, or a cold detachment in the face of other people's suffering or anxiety. What has happened is that such a leader is emotionally 'full'. Like a glass that is already brimming over, her capacity for emotion is exhausted by her own unmet needs and there is no space left for anyone else's. When she is faced with another person's unresolved emotions, instead of having the capacity to deal with them, she finds that her own emotions simply overflow onto the front stage.

An alternative to a leak is an explosion. The emotional control that is required to suppress your own emotions so that you can stay focused on other people's is like the plug in the top of a volcano. As the pressure builds inside, it takes more and more effort to keep the lid on, until one day it blows and the years of resentment pour out.

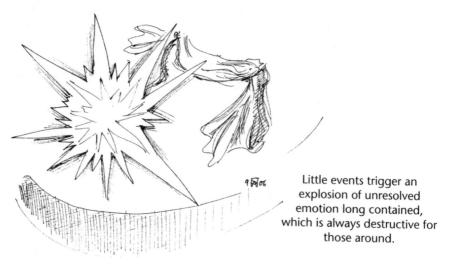

Little events trigger an explosion of unresolved emotion long contained, which is always destructive for those around.

A third option is collapse. In this case, the burden of sustaining the frontstage performance simply becomes too heavy. There is not enough strength or energy to keep it up. The exhausted leader struggles on long after he should have taken a break, driven on by the expectations of his audience (which includes, in all probability, stakeholders and shareholders demanding a higher return on their investment), until there is nothing left. His script is too tired, the props are too old. His back stage has not been able to renew them because it has been given no time or attention or resources. It is a shambles, and so one day the whole performace just falls apart. The actor has no more to give. The show can't go on.

Throughout the 1990s, one of the most highly respected preachers in Britain was a Baptist pastor I shall call 'Philip'. He led a large church in England, attended by hundreds of students and young professionals. He built a reputation for arresting and incisive Bible teaching, sharp argument and compelling rhetoric, and he was in great demand at major conferences. His line was essentially orthodox and conservative on all matters of faith and morality. Then, one day in 1998, apparently without warning, Philip left his wife and children and moved in with a male friend. Out of the blue, he severed his links with his previous existence, his previous identity, his previous role, his relationships and his beliefs. He turned his back on all that his life had meant for 50 years and embarked on an utterly new and different life, much of which contradicted what he had been hitherto. All that had mattered to him was overturned in one day. In one catastrophic revolution, he broke all the commitments he had made: of emotion, of covenant, of promise, of faith, of contract.

The collapse of a leader can destroy their attempts to maintain distinct front and back stages. Everything becomes visible and vulnerable.

What was it that brought him to this point, where he saw no other way forward than to destroy the life he had poured himself into for five decades? Of course I can't answer that question. But we can speculate about some of the circumstances in Philip's life that contributed to this breakdown. One of these was the frontstage performance that his audience had required him to give all those years. Obviously, he must have struggled with his sexuality for many years. Doubts about his orientation, awareness of his sexual needs, as well as confusion about Christian teaching, must have occupied his back stage for years. He must have expended enormous energy merely to keep his back stage secret, to prevent anyone even glimpsing it. And in order to do so, perhaps, he had pushed himself to perform even harder and better and more fluently on his front stage: to defend orthodoxy even more rigorously, to model the very highest ideals of the conformity his audience needed to see. He may have done so to convince not just them but also himself, to try to persuade himself that he really could hold on to this idealized life and its values. And, as he did so, day by day he must have buried his unresolved issues further and further backstage.

Philip never succeeded in finding a way to bring these things onto his front stage. He never managed to find a few confidants he could take backstage, to share with them the mess and pain and confusion and begin to address his anxieties. Maybe no one ever offered; maybe he thought that no one would accept him if they knew; maybe he felt he would be instantly judged and would fall from grace. And so he learned to separate his back stage from his front stage and become two people. I don't know what life must have been like for him during those years—the disjuncture between who everyone perceived him to be and who he knew himself to be growing wider every day. And then one day it simply all became too much, and the show was over.

The consequences were devastating, of course—and, like many others in the audience, I am in part to blame. As a young student at the time, sitting at his feet, so to speak, I asked him to stand on that pedestal. I expected him to model the perfect life. I denied him permission to be honest about his doubts. I didn't want him to deal with them, because I didn't want to deal with my own. My life was fraught with complexity and I wanted to simplify it, and I needed him to live a life that offered me clarity, hope and vision. I kept him frontstage while his life backstage collapsed. I, and many thousands of others in Britain.

What lies behind the creation of a front and a back stage is the sense that we can't entirely trust our audience, and so we need to manage what they see of us. I can remember the relief when I finally came clean to my congregation about what was going on in my back stage. As it happened, this was precipitated by a crisis, but for which I might have remained hidden away backstage. My wife, Jo, had just lost a baby in pregnancy (having nearly lost our firstborn) and then our second son contracted meningitis at just eight weeks old. I myself was struggling to manage the reins of the large church I found myself leading. Having been brought up to keep my emotional needs to myself, I did my best to hold things together, not letting on what was really happening. Jo would despair when I sank into the sofa in a dark, morose silence, having just made myself perform as the confident church leader at the front. The darkness deepened until I descended into full-blown clinical depression for nearly two years, and had several months signed off work.

Eventually, I cried out for help and allowed people to come backstage. I reckoned I had no choice—if I didn't do it, I would end up doing something I would live to regret. Jo remembers vividly overhearing one church member saying, 'What a shame! We had such high hopes for Simon as a bishop.' When we make ourselves vulnerable, we risk rejection and judgement. Such comments were rare, however, and in the main my experience was that many other people began to confide in me their own failings, doubts and discouragements. There was an increase of honesty, acceptance and respect in our community. My admission of my weakness gave others permission to admit their own.

People only become undefended when they feel safe. For me, it was a watershed. The burden was lifted and I no longer had to play the role of a superhero. I had begun to discover the road to freedom.

Freedom comes when we start to allow people to see not only the glossy image but the mess as well.

This also means that our back stage ceases to be a place of fear, containing all the mess that we avoid, and instead becomes available for fruitful exploration.

Study questions 3

1. Use the diagram below to illustrate what you put on your front and back stage. Consider such things as your relationships, your emotions, your achievements, your needs and so on.

2. In what ways do you experience...
   · leakage between back and front stage?
   · explosion?
   · collapse?
3. How does trust influence the development of your back stage and your front stage?
   · 'People I trust I take onto my ... stage.'
   · 'People I don't trust I keep on my ... stage.'

FOUR

Strategies of Defence II: Power

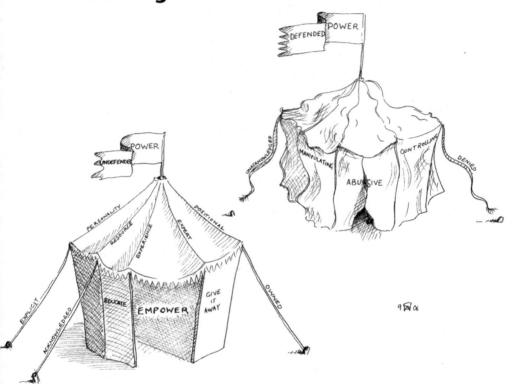

When you met him, it was like being caught off guard by a curve ball. No matter how much you prepared, you found yourself on the defensive in a matter of seconds. Tony was one of those people who somehow just seemed to know something about you or your situation that you wouldn't have expected. He had no right to know what he did, but somehow he did. Not that it was always threatening, mind you—often it would be, 'Simon, happy birthday for last week! How was London?' (How did he know I'd been to London to celebrate?) 'Simon! You're looking well—must have been the sun in Spain!' (How did he know where we'd been on holiday?) 'Simon, congratulations! You must be delighted to have won that contract!' (How on earth did he know I'd even gone for it?)

Tony made it his business to know things, and he had an uncanny ability to use what he knew at just the right time. I don't know if he intended it this way, but the effect was to unsettle you—leave you feeling a little surprised, exposed. What else did he know about you? Was nothing hidden? It meant you began the conversation, as I say, on the back foot. He had the initiative. He had set the agenda, and you were following it. By the time you had caught up with him, he was off somewhere else. Whatever you wanted to talk about, somehow you never set the terms for the encounter. Maybe it is no surprise that Tony was one of the most influential men in the region. A successful businessman, a respected industry figure—he made things happen. Tony had power, but more than one kind of power. He certainly had financial power, but he also had power that was due to his personality and his position.

In fact, as Charles Handy has suggested in his book *Understanding Organizations*, there are many kinds of power, and all of us have some power of some kind. For example, there is *personality power*. Research into the neuroscience of emotion has revealed how people are affected emotionally by others around them. The most effective leaders, by and large, are the most affective. This is because affective leaders influence the emotional state of their audience very strongly. They do this through the empathy (a cognitive ability about which we will talk at greater length later) that enables them to tune into and understand other people's emotional states. Leaders affect others because they resonate with them—an emotional chord is struck, and there is harmony. Moreover, effective leaders have developed the ability, whether through training or otherwise, to exploit social and emotional signalling to influence the emotional states of others. The body language of smiling and eye contact, listening posture, proximity, volume and tone of voice, pace and rhythm of speech, vocabulary, confidence, warmth, enthusiasm—these are the tools of personality power. On a power audit, most effective leaders score very high on their personality power. It is this that enables them to influence others to trust them, believe in them and follow them.

Second, there is *resource power*. This is to do with your ability to affect the success or failure of an operation because you have leverage with regard to the resources it needs—whether you control them yourself or have influence over others who do. The resources may be financial, technical, bureaucratic or some other kind. A person with resource power can make or break an operation simply by providing or withholding the resources required. A leader always needs to have some element of resource power, because without it the necessary means to 'make the journey' will not be available.

Third, there is *experience power*. This is the power that is acquired simply by being in a situation for a long time. Many a new initiative is stopped dead by the committee member who raises their eyebrows at the latest suggestion and quietly points out that some 20 years ago just such an idea was tried—and failed. Someone once said that experience is the comb life gives you after you have lost your hair. However, those who own the comb are usually pretty eager to use it on others with a fuller crop.

Fourth, there is *expert power*, which derives from having a greater degree of relevant expertise than your colleagues. Experts are usually brought in on any challenge or project that is technically difficult, and their knowledge and insight gives them technical power in that situation. By and large, the leader is not the greatest expert in every—or even any—situation, and so he will make use of others' expertise, and often defer to it on a consultancy basis.

Fifth, there is *positional power*. This is the power that is acquired simply by dint of being appointed to a position of authority within an organization. Since the system has legitimated this authority, there are certain executive decisions you can make. Related to positional power, as 'underneath' is related to 'from above', is *given power*. Whereas positional power is conferred by your superiors, given power is ascribed from below, by your followers. In other words, we are talking about the power gained through trust. The most powerful leaders usually have a high degree of both positional and given power. Indeed, often problems arise in leadership when there is a discrepancy between the power from below and the power from above—when the level of trust does not match the level of positional authority.

There are other kinds of power—physical power and spiritual power, for example—but what concerns us here is the fact that leaders wield power. By definition, influence is power—an ability to effect change. Whether it is a push or a pull, from above or from below, influence must involve power. What we must realize is that power is a pragmatic thing—in itself, it has no value attached to it. It is neither good nor bad to be powerful: the issue is how power is used. It is a question of praxis. The other thing we must appreciate is that power is a commodity. It is something that is possessed. You can accumulate power. You can accumulate personality power through developing social skills, resource power through hard work, experience power through longevity, expert power through education. Power is an asset that, over time, can be bought. And likewise it can be lost—taken away or given away. We give away power, for example, when we teach someone else something. The mother who teaches her child how to cook not only empowers the child but, in so doing, gives some of her own power away. Previously, there was a huge discrepancy in power between the mother and her child in this domain, but as she teaches the child, so the discrepancy grows smaller. As the child becomes more competent at cooking, so the mother loses some of her dominance. Thus, we should think of power as an asset—and recognize that, like all assets, there are many things you can do with it. Power can be spent, invested, multiplied, lost, given away, bought, sold and so on.

Most leaders have more power than others around them, and often they have a rich mixture of the six different kinds of power discussed above. The question is: What are they doing with all this power? When I speak at conferences, I often get delegates to make a simple audit of the power they actually possess in their roles. The audit considers their positional power, their experience power, their personality power, their resource power and their expert power, and also their spiritual power. Sometimes it comes as a surprise to people to discover that they probably have a lot more power than they thought. Older leaders sometimes feel that the reins are slipping from their hands, and they fail to see how much power they can exert in a planning meeting simply by dropping in the remark, 'Back in '75, we tried something very similar to that. I have to say it never really took off.' Such a comment, loaded with the weight of so much experience, can deter many a young leader from attempting something bold.

I was working with a school where the head teacher was trying to change the culture into something more collaborative. A staff meeting agreed that this new approach was a good thing, but, even with training, nothing changed. When I walked into the staffroom I sensed very quickly that the blockage was one individual: the deputy head. Clara had been on the staff longer than anyone else, and was well known and liked by the parents. Despite frequent opportunities, she had never applied to be head, preferring (as she put it) not to have all the pressure of the administration and management. Now, without ever explicitly challenging the head's plans, she was simply being very passive. The effect on the staff was slowly to drain away all their energy and confidence. I began to see that Clara had no desire to embrace change herself—she was comfortable as she was—and she was preventing it simply by remaining disengaged, by dint of her long experience and her popularity with parents. Her 'buy-in' was needed to make something happen. Otherwise, all she had to do was do nothing and nothing would change.

Sometimes, the unacknowledged power in a system can be used more positively than this. I was nurtured as a teenager in an organization in which mentoring played a major role. The mentors were usually impressive figures, whose devotion and conviction were evident to all. Unconsciously, we all aspired to impress them and be like them. Indeed, I suspect that we feared their rebuke or rejection. It was amazing how our attitudes on many issues—how we should spend our holidays, which books we should read, which university we should go to, whether or not we should get married—were determined by the unspoken opinions of these people. Officially, there was openness on all these questions, but in practice there was a clear hierarchy of values and, one after another, the choices we actually made were almost identical. In this system, power was located not so much in any obvious contract of authority as, invisibly, in the way we idealized our mentors and needed to belong and be accepted. This kind of power can derive not only from the charisma of the leaders but from the tradition of the institution as well.

I can remember how my own power was pointed out to me after I had chaired a student union meeting at university. An older and wiser postgraduate student, who used to come along to support me, took me aside and asked me whether I was aware how much power I had over the group. He explained to me that anything I said carried a lot of weight, and on reflection I could see he was right. Without realizing it, I had taken into that meeting expert, positional and personality power which had all combined to make my contribution to the discussion hard for others to oppose. No wonder decisions tended to fall my way! I also had to acknowledge the uncomfortable truth that there was something in me that enjoyed this dominance and was happy to exploit it. As a result of that insight, I often tell leaders now to 'tread lightly' when they express an opinion—they must appreciate the extra weight it will carry simply by being theirs.

Experts speak of the 'psychological contract' that exists in any organization. By this, they mean that there is something else, informal and often unacknowledged, besides the financial or structural contract that determines expectations and rewards. In a tight, familial organization, this may revolve around a single figure, an archetypal 'parent' who the 'children' feel they ought to please and emulate. In larger organizations, it can consist in the obligation you feel to 'the firm' or 'the vision'. This is often particularly the case when the 'mission' is a social, ethical or spiritual one. In one of the organizations I have worked for, we used to talk about how 'for the sake of the work' we gave up doing things we would otherwise choose to do, acknowledging that the 'mission' took precedence over our personal freedoms. 'For the sake of the work' can invoke duty and sacrifice, but it can also be used to bully legitimate objections into submission.

One of the biggest issues that have preoccupied thinkers and commentators in recent decades has been that of the ethics of power. Through the work primarily of Michel Foucault, we have become very aware of the reality and the dynamics of power in any situation. Concerns over the abuse of power have been crucial to the debates over racism and sexism, equal opportunities, gay rights and rights for disabled people, globalization, institutional religion and many other social issues of our day. In effect, we have been experiencing a sea change in the balances of power over the past four decades, and it is not finished yet.

Foucault insisted that there is always power exercised in any situation, and therefore the most dangerous kind of power is unacknowledged power. When it goes underground, when it is not recognized and owned, power becomes a liability, just as dynamite becomes a liability unless it is handled carefully and knowingly and certain safety procedures are observed. Just as it can be lethal for someone with explosive to deny—or even not be aware—that they were in possession of it, so it is with power. The most dangerous kind of person is the one with a great deal of power who denies that they have any, or who denies that power is a fundamental factor in their leadership. This is the strategy of what I call 'defended' leaders.

The undefended leader, on the other hand, does all she can to acknowledge her exercise of power, and the flow of power in her organization, and to make them both explicit and accountable.

Study questions 4

1. Rate yourself on a scale of 1–10 according to how much of these five different kinds of power you feel you exercise in your leadership:
   - Personality
   - Resource
   - Experience
   - Expert
   - Positional

2. Add up your total score, out of a possible 50. This will give you some indication of how much power you think you currently possess as a leader.

3. Is this total score more or less than you may have expected?

4. In what ways do you use your power positively in your leadership?
   - to educate and train others?
   - to help and protect the vulnerable?
   - to empower projects around you?
   - to improve the potential of the organization?

5. Are there any people in your organization who, in your opinion, possess power without realizing it? What is the impact of such people? What could you do to help them become more aware of the impact they may be having on others?

FIVE

Strategies of Defence III: Control

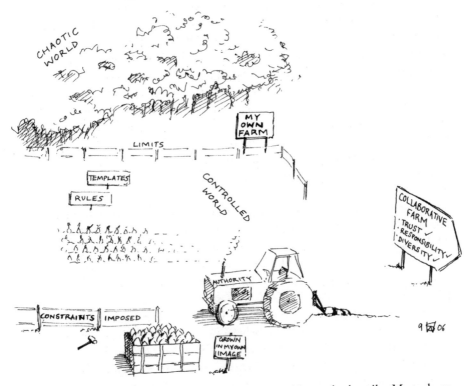

The world is an unpredictable and risky place, and it can be hostile. My task, as a human being, is to find a way to be safe in it, and one of the ways I achieve that is through control. Control offers us a sense of security—but it is perhaps wise to recognize that it is really only an illusion of security. Ultimately, nothing we have the power to do can make us truly safe. However, that does not stop me trying. For example, if I control my diary I feel secure that nothing is going to trip me up unexpectedly. If I control my money, I feel that I am protected from financial crisis and penury. If I control my followers, I feel that the project I am leading will be protected from failure. If I control what I eat, I feel that I am not merely at the mercy of overwhelming circumstances or anxieties I cannot control.

All of us use mechanisms of control, and at times these are entirely appropriate. It is appropriate to exercise control over a child when they are about to run into the road. It is appropriate for the surgeon to exercise control over an assistant who is about to slice through a major artery by mistake. It is appropriate for the authorities to exercise control over a violent criminal who would otherwise commit further crimes. Control is not in itself a bad thing. In times of crisis, when the consequences of not being in control would be disastrous, exerting control is appropriate, necessary and good.

However, wanting to be in control can become a highly destructive disorder. Obsessive-compulsive disorder, or OCD, is increasingly recognized and highlighted as an example of the way a mechanism of control can become ritualized and embedded in a very damaging way. Some people, when faced with an unresolvable concern that cannot be controlled, relieve their sense of impotence and anxiety by focusing on another, arbitrary behaviour over which they can exercise control. Unconsciously, they choose a surrogate, whether it be washing their hands, not touching people unless they're wearing gloves or whatever, and this becomes a ritual that, when engaged in, releases a certain neurochemical that soothes them. However, OCD works in much the same way as any other addiction: it offers comfort, but at a great cost. It requires loyalty and obedience. It demands attention. It occupies, and preoccupies, the mind as a craving without which you are not safe. It gives less and less reward, while insisting that more and more is sacrificed.

OCD is typically addressed, in Britain's National Health Service, through cognitive behavioural therapy, or CBT, which seeks to unlearn the neural pathways that direct the repetitive, obsessive behaviour. While only a small percentage of people suffer from acute OCD, a much higher percentage of people exhibit at least some of the behaviours that could develop into this kind of self-soothing control. One of the things I do when I feel anxious or dejected is to listen to the same track on a CD over and over again, maybe 10 or 20 times or more without stopping. I find the repetition soothing: it offers me a rhythm of predictability, it takes me into a world where I know what is coming next, where I can escape the pressure of the disorder of life around me. Listening to a track repeatedly is one of my mechanisms for sustaining an illusion of control during a period of stress. I notice how children love the repetition of characters, storylines and formats in the shows they watch, which I am sure offers them the same comfort of familiarity. For others, it will be something different. My wife will often embark on a good spring clean when she feels anxious, and she tells me that many of her friends do the same. Other people keep lists, others obsess about their health, others may insist on having everything 'just so' in their office, or on having a cigarette every evening after work (which creates its own addiction) or a glass of wine or two, or on looking at pornography.

Control offers us an illusion of escape from the chaotic world we inhabit into a constructed reality in which there is order and predictability. In general, as human beings we need to feel soothed in order to feel well, and being in control is a mechanism to achieve this. Much of our quest for control, therefore, is not actually a response to stress or crisis—mostly, we exercise control in order to make the world more familiar to us. The result of this is that we will tend to try to construct a world around us that resonates with our own personal needs. If we can achieve this, we will feel safer; we will find ourselves inhabiting a world we understand, which we can predict and interpret. It is much safer for me to inhabit my own world than to inhabit yours. I don't know you as well as I know myself; I don't trust you as much as I trust myself. So, I decide that a world shaped in my own image is my best option.

This desire to create a world in our own image in order to feel safely in control is common to all of us. However, the leader is in a unique position to achieve this desire. Being in leadership gives you the authority, the power and the resources to structure your environment. A leader has the positional power to make changes, to dictate timing and establish rhythms and determine what happens when and how. Unlike most people, who have to make the best of a world someone else has shaped, the leader can set her own rules within her particular domain. It should be no great surprise, therefore, how often you find that the personality of an organization reflects the personality of its leader.

Jeremy—not his real name—is the head teacher of an independent day school in England for 400 eight-to-thirteen-year-olds. When you visit the school, you immediately pick up a sense of focused, slightly manic energy. The children move swiftly from one activity to another; they are always on the go, always advancing towards some goal. The school is efficient, formal yet modern. The staff are motivated. Expectations are high—including standards of appearance. When you walk round with Jeremy, he is constantly spotting a pupil with a tie loose or a button undone. He will know where each of the 400 children should be at any time of day, and often will know some particular fact about them that day. He always knows more than his staff about what should be happening and when.

Jeremy has been at the school for many years as head. He would say of himself that he knows everything there is to know and that way he is in control—he will never be caught out. His roving eye is never off the ball. Like the Dark Lord in *The Lord of the Rings*, there is no corner of the school where his gaze does not penetrate. His appearance is immaculate, his manners impeccable; his eyes hold yours in a fixed stare that challenges you to find any trace of disorder.

Inevitably, Jeremy finds any kind of threat to his control deeply problematic, especially if it comes in the form of an equally competent, equally experienced colleague who sees things differently.

Paul—not his real name—is the leader of a large church in England. It doesn't take you long to realize what a busy and exciting place this church is. There are dozens of children's groups, midweek activities, courses on marriage and parenting, evangelism and outreach. There are special mission weeks, children's clubs in the summer, weekends away, men's groups, women's groups, pensioner groups, homework groups. There is work in schools, work in deprived areas of the city, work the church funds in Africa, Asia, Russia and South America. The church is alive with visitors and newcomers, and overrun with children. Its services can feel like a trip to a funfair, as you are bombarded with sensations that leave you somewhat dizzy.

Here are some of the things Paul would say about himself. He finds it quite hard to be on his own. He finds it a challenge to pray privately and silently. He finds it hard to be doing nothing. He is tempted to avoid looking at the difficult stuff in his life. Other people would say of Paul that he is a fantastically confident, secure leader, always open to new opportunities, always looking forward.

Denise—not her real name—was the principal of a college in England that trained future teachers. The college had a reputation for academic excellence and prided itself on its scholarly rigour. At first glance, it was not entirely clear who was the leader of the college: the principal was often away, lecturing abroad, and responsibility was devolved to the vice-principals. When Denise was there, she was often buried in her office writing papers or books. Access to her was by appointment; informal chance meetings in corridors or at the dinner table were brief, as she struggled with small talk. Direction to the college was typically given via 'set pieces'—prepared lectures, valedictory dinners or other staged and formal events at which she could make a presentation. Decisions were made not by the principal but by the entire staff—some 18 people—who would have to come to some kind of consensus on every issue. Inevitably, decision-making was slow and often convoluted. The college was full of mature students preparing for a life in education, busily engaged in academic learning but paying rather less attention to their practical training and social skills. Often, students left the college feeling that they had made less progress emotionally or practically than academically in their time there.

Jeremy, Paul and Denise: three leaders of three different organizations. Yet in each case there is a close correspondence between their personality as leader and the personality of the organization they lead. In each case, it could fairly be said that if you wanted to know what the leader was like, you should look at the community around them. Their organization was, if you like, a projection of their personality onto the larger screen of an institution or society. The characteristics of the lives of each of these three individuals had become manifest in the character of the culture around them. That culture was like a human sculpture, fashioned by the things that drove them personally, including their needs and fears as well as their values and ideals.

For Jeremy, the culture reflected his need to be in control, to feel that he was always achieving standards and goals. It expressed his own internal struggles to live with failure and accept compromise, and his anxiety about his own competence. His demand for achievement from his pupils was a projection of the demands he made of himself. His school was his frontstage performance; and, like his own, its back stage was well hidden, in case it might spoil the immaculate polish out front.

For Paul, the culture reflected his need to be busy, always forward-looking, always on his front stage. It expressed the struggle to be still that he experienced in himself, the discomfort about 'doing nothing'. It expressed his desire for activity and growth. In Goffman's terms, it had, just like Paul, a front stage that was full of high energy and a back stage that was highly underdeveloped.

For Denise, the culture reflected her need for space and personal autonomy, and her avoidance in her own life of emotional language and the social engagement that made her feel insecure. Her demand that her students should focus on academic work was a projection of her desire to concentrate in her own life on the areas where she felt most competent. Denise vacated the front stage of the organization because that is what she did in her own personal life—she had not developed the confidence to perform comfortably out front. Set-piece presentations were the only realistic way to bring out onto the front stage of the college some of the ideas she had been beavering away over backstage.

Often, we discuss the issue of control in terms of the 'control freak': the person who has to micromanage everything, with eyes everywhere and fingers in every pie. Of course, that is one expression of control; but I am suggesting that the exertion of control is more complex and much more common than this. No leader is free from exerting control in order to create a world in which they feel safe—and, unlike others, the leader has the opportunity actually to take control. Once again, as with power, it is healthy for a leader to recognize and acknowledge their exertion of control and make it explicit. Control is one of the least acknowledged defences of the leader, and it is what often prevents them from working collaboratively with others. Collaboration always involves creating space for other people genuinely to express themselves. It is like allowing other actors on the stage to perform besides you. Attempts at genuine collaboration always fail if they merely require the other person slavishly to follow your script and your stage direction. Only when the leader is willing to follow someone else's script can collaboration truly be said to be taking place.

In October 1991, Linus Torvalds, a computer-science postgraduate student at the University of Helsinki, announced on the Internet that he had written a 'free version of a minix-lookalike for AT-386 computers' and would make it available to anyone who was interested. For the non-technical, Torvalds had created an alternative operating system to Microsoft Windows, the system that probably runs your computer. Unlike Windows, Linux (as he named his system) is what is called 'open-source' software. In other words, it is free—you don't have to buy it. Furthermore, you could, if you wanted to and had the ability, contribute to its next edition. The software has been written almost entirely by a growing group of volunteer programmers—hackers, for want of a better word—who responded to Torvalds' invitation to 'join in'. By the end of 1998, more than 264,000 lines of code had been written and more than eight million users were running Linux on a wide variety of platforms.

That year, it was estimated that Linux accounted for 17 per cent of server operating systems and it was projected to see a compound annual growth-rate of 25 per cent, two-and-a-half times greater than the rest of the market. Linux was widely regarded as being of very high quality and very reliable. In both 1997 and 1998, it won the InfoWorld award for the best operating system, and in 1997 it also won the InfoWorld award for best technical support. By 2007, it is estimated that Linux will have taken some 37 per cent of the market.[5]

But the real fascination with Linux stems from the fact that it is not the product of an organization. In its earliest years, no systems group developed the design, no management board approved the plan, the budget and the schedule, no HR department hired the programmers. Instead, volunteers from all over the world contributed code, documentation and technical support over the Internet, just because they wanted to.

Linux is a story of distributed work and collaborative leadership. Torvalds himself still exercises editorial control over the script that is contributed, and there is now a management structure in place to support the much more complex relationships between authors, editors and customers. However, the shape of the software represents the vision of a community rather than an individual. In order to achieve this, Torvalds had to take the risk of allowing others to play a leading role—literally to write the script. It involved creating the mechanisms for their contributions to be recognized and incorporated; it involved an openness to the future and an emergent approach to the market.

---

[5] Jae Yun Moon and Lee Sproull, 'Essence of Distributed Work: The Case of the Linux Kernel', *First Monday*, vol 5 no 11 (November 2000)—posted at http://firstmonday.org/issues/issue5_11/moon/index.html

It involved flexibility and also, dare I say it, humility on Torvalds' part. This is the case not least in terms of financial ambition: Linux makes its money from service partnerships, whereby it charges a fee for managing, maintaining and updating its system. Torvalds himself is no Bill Gates, paying himself only a modest $200,000 a year.

I suspect that many of us, reading this, will find ourselves admiring this achievement but also recognizing how immensely challenging we ourselves would find it to lead our organization in this way. Allowing others to be in control where appropriate may be the hallmark of the undefended leader, but that doesn't make it any the less difficult!

Leading in our own image

This is my proposition: all of us create worlds in our own image, but the difference for leaders is that they have the positional authority to do so. If I am right in this, then it is vital for leaders to appreciate that they have the mandate and the power to impose their personality on the community around them. Within the environment over which we have authority and for which we have responsibility (be it a family, a classroom, an office, a voluntary society or the boardroom of a global multinational), we impose our own personal strategy on those around us and seek to create a world that meets our own needs. The community becomes an extension of us, and our followers become performers on our stage, using our script to tell our story. There is an identification of the person of the leader with the performance of the organization they lead.

For us, therefore, there is a moral responsibility and an ethical imperative to know ourselves, not for our own benefit but for the benefit of our followers. And not only to know ourselves but to be free from our selves. It is freedom that is the critical factor: freedom to make decisions and choose courses of action that in the end may lead to personal loss rather than personal gain. I have suggested already that this moral freedom is a characteristic of all undefended leaders.

In contrast, leaders who cling to personal power and are not free always, in the end, become corrupted. Robert Mugabe, the senior executives of Enron and WorldCom—these are men who are (or were) ultimately enslaved, whose leadership of their country or company became inextricably bound up with their own personal status and ambition. Their willingness to lead their followers down the road to disaster stemmed from their slavery to their own personal needs, which they had to use their society or organization to satisfy.

If we are not free, our organization is not free. If we are still captive to our own need to achieve, to gain personal reputation and standing, wealth and influence, the organization will always be subjected to our personal strategy to accomplish this. We may wriggle and squirm to avoid this conclusion, but we can't. We may desperately want to soften it—to say that, true, some leaders become too self-interested, but a little self-interest is fine; but we must face the reality. The truth is that, until we are set free from the need to get a favourable response from our audience, everyone concerned, leaders and followers, will be trapped.

It is for this reason that civilized countries have established over the centuries checks and balances to curb the power and autonomy of their leaders. They recognize the potential for corruption in leadership and so they limit their leaders' freedom to perform their own script under their own direction. We set political and legal constraints round our leaders to prevent them from becoming dictators. The worst of the world's leaders are those who dismantle such constraints in order to give themselves more freedom. Almost invariably the temptations are too great, even for those who start out with high ideals and noble aspirations. Accountability and submission are crucial factors in leadership: no leader should be without them.

However, such constraints are not enough in themselves. They are designed to limit the damage a leader may do, but they cannot help to make a leader free within themself. We have seen in history leaders whose lives were set free from personal need and aspiration. These are the women and men who had the moral courage to take the hard road, and invite their followers to take it with them, not because it would make them rich or successful but because it was the only way to freedom. And it is to this kind of leadership and this kind of life we are called to aspire. In the end, it is about being undefended as a human being so that you can be undefended as a leader.

Our pursuit of undefended leadership must take us further into the journey to find how to live an undefended life.

Study questions 5

1. When you feel you have lost control, what strategies do you employ to regain it?
2. What strategies do you use to exert control in your leadership?
3. In what ways does the organization (or team or department or whatever) that you lead reflect your personality?
4. How does this enable you to feel in control?
5. What examples of genuinely collaborative leadership have you seen?
6. What did the leaders do to make that happen?
7. We often discover how free we are only when we lose the things we have. What things would you find it hard to lose?
   - Reputation
   - Status
   - Income
   - Popularity
   - Role
   - Power
   - Autonomy
   - Control

Part II

LOCATING THE ROOTS OF THE DEFENDED SELF

SIX

Our Experience of Trust

9 ☒ 06

To understand the route to undefendedness, we must first understand the architecture of our ego, for ultimately it is that that we are defending. The ego is formed throughout childhood. Research suggests that there are two periods of childhood when our ego is most plastic. The first is in early childhood, when we are shaped by our parents; the second is in adolescence, when we are shaped by our peers. These periods coincide with times when our hormones make us open and impressionable, when the 'hard wiring' of our brains is more flexible and we retain experiences and memories in their architectural structure. Most important, these times coincide with periods when we are forming our attachments with our significant others.

John Bowlby's work has been seminal in developing an appreciation of the role of trust in forming our ego. Trust is, to put it simply, the degree to which you can rely upon a relationship. It is like a rope between two people: how strong the trust is determines the weight it can bear. Bowlby's basic theory is that children need to grow up attached to others by strong ropes. There is no secure attachment without trust, and it is such secure attachments that form us and give us a safe, reliable, predictable environment in which to grow.[6]

The reason that trust is so important to the formation of the ego is to do with danger. We need to appreciate just how threatening the world is, especially to a small child, surrounded by what seem like powerful giants, any one of whom can hurt them. When we are small, we are vulnerable and need protecting. Our 'ropes' protect us: they give us limits and they also mean we are attached to powerful figures who can fight on our behalf. Without these ropes, the growing child soon feels vulnerable and anxious and has to find other ways to protect themselves. The child psychologist Margot Sunderland has suggested that these ways can include being aggressive and bullying in order to appear strong. They may also include being compliant. They may involve being the class fool who does anything to win the favour of the crowd. In the absence of strong ropes, children resort to a mixture of what psychologists call 'self-holding' and 'self-promoting' in order to make themselves secure. Such patterns of behaviour, developed in early life, are robust and remarkably difficult to change.

Mark had been a community leader for many years. He had tremendous insight into his faith and strong convictions about the role of the community in society; and yet he would often be told that he lacked confidence and appeared indecisive in his leadership. Something was preventing him from expressing clearly and strongly on his front stage the values and ideas that enthused him on his back stage. He had grown up in a household with a dominating father who, while not a cruel or unkind man, could be dismissive and on occasion aggressive. As an imaginative and sensitive teenager, Mark learned to keep his thoughts private rather than take the risk of expressing them on his front stage. The threat of his ideas being belittled or ignored was too great. It was safer to keep them to himself because he couldn't trust his father's reaction.

---

[6] John Bowlby, *Attachment and Loss* (New York: Basic Books, vol 1 1969, vol 2 1973, vol 3 1980)

Despite being a grown man now in his fifties, with children of his own, Mark had retained his expectation that the 'audience' to which he had to present his ideas might be dismissive. Somehow, the experience he had had as a teenager had become applied to his relationships in general. As a result, his leadership had suffered from a lack of decisive confidence in articulating his ideas.

Mark developed a small front stage with few of the leadership skills needed to communicate his ideas.

Mark's back stage became a place of safety, where he protected himself by cultivating his thinking, and managing his emotion, so that he was fortified against criticism.

Craig had grown up as the youngest of five. His older siblings would frequently treat him as the baby, laughing at anything he said or did, carelessly putting him down, as teenagers can often do, without thought for the effect it might have. Now he was an adult, his relationship with them was much improved—indeed, they now regarded him as someone with wisdom who they would go to in a crisis. Nonetheless, Craig was left with a legacy. He would often let other people dominate conversation, and would defer to strong characters even when he had an opinion. He would fume that others would talk over him in a discussion, and yet he would never be able to find the courage to tell them they were out of order. He told me that it felt as if he was hiding just behind the curtain of his stage.

Craig became nervous and deferential in groups, because he predicted that his contribution would be laughed at.

When he came out, he expected to be greeted with jeers and laughter from an audience that would mock and belittle whatever he had to say. It simply wasn't worth the risk, so instead he had developed a deferential performance, designed to secure at least a non-hostile reaction from the crowd. Somehow, the experience Craig had had as a child had been transferred to his relationships with other people in general, even though his relationships with his siblings in particular were now much better.

Sarah went to boarding school, an environment in which weakness was instantly picked on and exploited. She learned that in order to survive she needed to give a performance of confidence and humour. She developed a quick repartee and was always at the centre of the action. As an adult, she was a master of deflection: if anything came too close for comfort, she would use her humour to bat it away, shielding any vulnerability she might have. As a leader, she was always preoccupied with what others might be thinking of her and how she could manage their impressions. Her experience of a hostile peer-group at school had been transferred to her adult peers, with the result that she expected other people to take advantage of anything she might give away of a personal nature, unless she remained in control of the encounter.

Sarah developed a large front stage, to which she devoted all her attention, to manage the impression the audience had of her and prevent them from turning against her.

Mark, Craig and Sarah are not unusual: I could relate literally hundreds of stories in which the experience of trust an individual had had as a child—both of being trusted and of finding others to be trustworthy—had determined their expectations of people in general when they had grown to adulthood. It seems as if the particular experiences of childhood become generalized and applied to everyone—even a negative experience that has since in some way been 'redeemed'. In his later work, in collaboration with another psychologist, Ingar Bretherton, Bowlby went on to propose a mechanism by which this transfer might occur. The suggestion is that in their early years children construct a working model of the way they expect that people will treat them, based on their experience of attachments.

There is a certain logic to this idea. As human beings, we have to learn how to make predictions, because we never know for sure what is going to happen even in the next 10 seconds. Certainly, when I walk into a room full of people I don't know precisely how they are going to react to me—in a sense, I am in the dark. However, my past experience of how people have treated me—and, most fundamentally, whether they have proved trustworthy or not—acts as a kind of 'psychological headlights'. I use the working model I constructed as a child predictively, to try to 'see' what is coming so I can be prepared. Mark, Craig and Sarah all developed ways to manage risk in a world in which other people could not always be trusted. When someone grows up in an environment in which those around *can* be trusted, the outcome may be very different.

Felicity grew up with parents who were consistent and reliable and who allowed her to take risks. They gave her an experience of being trusted. When she tried out her ideas in conversations, they were listened to and well received. Her audience—her parents—was essentially one that welcomed and valued all her performances. Felicity learned to trust herself on the stage, and she internalized the prediction that people would basically receive her well. She never really experienced people as threatening and so she didn't suffer from anxiety, because her working model predicted that people would probably give her a fair hearing. As an adult, she became known as a confident and secure leader who took risks and encouraged others to do so, too.

One of the factors that cause this transfer of early childhood experience into an adult working model of trust is the way the brain both forms and sorts memories. There are several regions of the brain involved in the laying down of memory, and each has a slightly different function. The memory I have of how I learned to kick a football, for example, is located in a different part of my brain from my memories of my greatest goals, which in turn are stored in a different place from the one that remembers *how* to kick a ball! The area of the brain that is associated with emotional memory in early years is very good at retaining the sensations we first experienced in any context—and the hormonal responses of fear or joy that went with them, such as a faster heart-rate, sweaty palms, dilated pupils. However, this area of the brain is very bad at discriminating which actual experience first evoked that emotional response. The actual explicit memory of that first occasion gets stored in a separate region of the brain, and the two areas do not 'talk' to each other very well. Not only that, but the memory of the occasion tends to decay quite rapidly whereas the sensations it produced linger on. The upshot of this is that we can recall—or be reminded of—powerful sensations and emotions from childhood without being able to remember what it was exactly that produced them. This means that a whole range of stimuli which may be quite different from the original can now trigger the same emotional reaction in us. To put it another way, the experience that triggers the emotional response becomes generalized from something very specific to something much more diffuse.[7]

It is in our early years in particular that we establish patterns of reaction to generalized stimuli that remind us, even inaccurately, of certain past experiences. The consequences of this way of forming memory is that early, sensory memories—for example, of fear—are retained and generalized, and resurface throughout our lives long after we have forgotten what it was that caused them. They exist as a kind of memory landscape, continuing to determine our emotional topography throughout our lives. The metaphor of a 'working model' conveys the idea that such memories, even if we are unconscious of them, may continue to inform the way we predict that people will treat us.

Explicit memories of events and experiences are laid down here but decay quite rapidly.	Analytical, explicit level of brain
Memories of sensations and emotions can flood back throughout our lives, triggered by apparently unrelated events.	Neural hinterland, where we re-experience old emotional memories
Sensory memories are stored elsewhere in the brain and are not connected to the memory of the actual event.	Emotional, sensory level of brain

Diagram 6.1   A schematic diagram illustrating the way the brain lays down explicit and emotional memories in two different, and poorly connected, areas

Over the past five years, I have worked intensively one-to-one with more than a hundred leaders. In the main, this has involved several sessions, totalling many hours, over a number of weeks or months. I have yet to come across a leader whose approach to leadership is not strongly informed by their early experiences as a child. This is not to say that it is always their parents who have shaped their behaviour. Siblings, peer groups at school, teachers and youth leaders and others can all have an influence. Nor is it to say that their genetic make-up has not had an impact—of course, it has. But invariably the root of the defendedness they exhibit as a leader, the strategy they use to make themselves

---

[7] Joseph LeDoux, *The Emotional Brain* (London: Phoenix, 1999)

safe, lies in the experience of trust they recorded as a child. Whether it is to compete, confront, negotiate or concede, the strategy they choose as an adult leader refers back to one they came to develop in their early years, in response to their experience of other people as trustworthy or otherwise. It is to these strategies we must now turn.

Study questions 6

1. What experience of being trusted did you have as a child?
2. Describe how, essentially, you expect people to react when you come out onto your front stage?

I expect that when I come onto my front stage people will...

- Is your working model basically one that trusts other people or one that does not?
- Have you had occasions when you suddenly felt powerful emotions that were apparently unrelated to anything that was happening at the time? If so, these were sensory memories that you had laid down at some stage in your past and had since generalized.

➲ On the website, www.theleadershipcommunity.org, are a number of 'visual landscaping' audio exercises. These were designed to help people to begin to become aware of and address their unconscious sensory memories, in a way that has proved powerful and useful for many. Try the exercises 'Creating your own landscape' and Exploring your landscape'. You need to be registered as a free 'guest member' in order to be able to listen to the audio exercises.

SEVEN

Our Response to Trust: The Shaping Leadership Ego—Over-Confidence and Paternalism

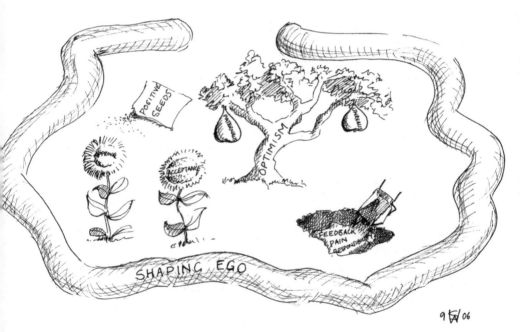

In 1991, two psychologists, Kim Bartholomew and Leonard M Horowitz, wrote a paper suggesting that there may be four different 'shapes' of ego that emerge out of different nurturing environments in infancy. The first type of ego, which they labelled *secure*, is gained by infants who have a positive view of both themselves and their caregivers. The second, which they labelled *dismissing*, is gained by those who receive over-intrusive care and as a result form a positive view of themselves but a negative one of their caregivers. The third, labelled *preoccupied*, is gained by those who fail to attract sufficient attention from their caregivers. This gives them a positive view of their caregivers but a negative view of themselves, and predisposes them to a preoccupation with trying to find secure emotional ties. The fourth type of ego, which Bartholomew and Horowitz labelled *fearful*, is gained by infants who receive unpredictable, disorientating care. This gives them a negative view of both themselves and their caregivers, predisposing them to fear being hurt.

What is interesting in these suggestions is the interplay between the infant's view of others and her view of herself. As children grow up, they try to make sense of what happens to them; and often a child will conclude that if something bad happens to them, it is because they themselves are bad and deserved it. If my parents are quarrelling, I may, as a child, conclude that it is something I have done that has made them fight—and if they split up, it is my fault: I am to blame. It is in the nature of the innate egoism of children to assume that they are the root cause of what they experience. This being the case, it is likely that a child will form a specific working model not only of other people but also of himself from the care he receives in childhood.

Let's look at this in relation to trust. Let's imagine the stories of four different individuals, each of whom choose a different way to cope with the trustworthiness or otherwise of the caregivers around them.

Imagine that a child grows up in a home in which she is trusted and supported. In Bowlby's terms, her attachments are secure. In this home, she receives approval and affection from a number of different caregivers—one or both parents, one or more close siblings, a formative teacher or whatever. I will refer to these caregivers as 'X'. The messages the child perceives from X are that she can trust both herself and, indeed, other people. Her experience is that other people are basically on her side, that they are reliable and, most important, that they are essentially safe.

Imagine this child's ego forming, rather like a landscape taking shape. At birth, the landscape is unformed and incoherent. But over time, as it is shaped by the influence of loving care around it, it begins to gain a boundary and a topography. The plants of approval and affirmation are sown; the borders of self-confidence and self-definition are marked out. Those caregivers who walk in this landscape do so with care and respect; they keep their word, they give encouragement, they are present and available.

As the child grows, she may develop the confidence and trust to allow others to come into her landscape, without fear that it will be trampled and damaged. Moreover, the boundaries and basic topography of that landscape formed in her early years will tend to prove robust and last for the rest of her life. While many other elements will be added, and some taken away, the fundamental character of her landscape, confident and strong, will probably endure. In short, her ego has a secure presence in the world.

High level of trust in self
High level of trust in others

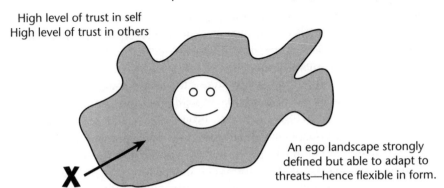

An ego landscape strongly
defined but able to adapt to
threats—hence flexible in form.

X

X perceived as unconditional and positive

Diagram 7.1   The pattern of the Shaping Ego

The Shaping Ego is one that perceives X to have been unconditional and positive. What develops from this is two characteristics: first, a high level of trust in themself; second, a high level of trust in others. Here is a self that tends to feel safe, that by and large hopes for and expects a positive response from other people. Many of us go through life managing a measure of anxiety—anxiety that probably stems from the unconscious expectation of some kind of threat (of failure, rejection, disapproval or the like). The Shaping Ego, in its caricature (which is what we are painting here to make the point), doesn't experience any such pervading anxiety. Life is essentially unthreatening, on two grounds: first, that you don't expect others to threaten you, and second, that even if you were threatened (by failure, rejection or disapproval, for example), it would not be catastrophic. Your sense of self is neither built upon nor destroyed by such things, and you would recover.

In Charles Dickens' novel *Bleak House*, John Jarndyce, the middle-aged master of the house in question, represents the best qualities of a Shaping Ego. Generous, trusting and forgiving, he has the care of two young wards, one of whom, Richard, seeks the settlement of a will that, he hopes, will make him immensely rich. In pursuing his claim, and against the advice of his guardian, Richard 'girds his means to the winds' and, tragically, dies penniless. Throughout, however, Jarndyce chooses not to give in to anger at the costly folly of his young ward; instead, he hopes the best for him, trusts him and supports him financially in his debts, despite Richard's resentment and distrust of his motives. At its best, the Shaping Ego is an optimistic and forgiving one, able to see and welcome the potential in others and to celebrate their successes.

Dickens also introduces to us another masterfully-drawn character, Mr Skimpole. He is a charming young fellow and a regular guest of Jarndyce who assures all he meets of his innocence. Like Jarndyce, he is not prone to judgementalism: he, too, is optimistic and forgiving of others' failings, seeing that he himself, as he tells us, 'is only a child'. However, his self-deprecation masks laziness and self-indulgence, ill discipline and lack of compassion. Skimpole has mastered the feat of never being worried or troubled by the plight of anyone, and he enjoys the goodwill and indulgence of those who overlook his selfishness on account of his charm, good humour and bonhomie. Ultimately, he is a callous character impossible to admire, whose overdeveloped view of himself is concealed behind politeness and apology. The Shaping Ego, at its worst, can be prone to self-indulgence and indifference. Sensitivity and compassion for the plight of others grow out of our own experience of anxiety, loss and sadness; and without such experience the Shaping Ego may be superficially warm but fundamentally cold, apparently concerned and yet, in reality, self-absolved of responsibility.

There is a lazy assumption widespread in the West that low self-esteem lies at the root of antisocial behaviour. Encouraged by the positive psychologies of the 1960s and '70s many people still believe that if only it were possible to give delinquent youths a more positive view of themselves, their antisocial and criminal behaviour would diminish. My wife works with emotionally and behaviourally dysfunctional children in schools and she finds that there is often a correlation between a negative, unstable and even dangerous home environment and a child's misbehaviour at school. However, it is interesting that, in a largescale review of research literature in 1996, Baumeister, Smart and Boden found that the evidence overwhelmingly contradicted the theory that low self-esteem causes violence.[8]

They observed this pattern present in people from playground bullies to abusive spouses to gang leaders to racist thugs to dictators: that the decisive cause of aggression and violence is not low self-esteem but a perceived threat to the ego. Contrary to popular belief, too much self-esteem can be a bad thing. Where it is exaggerated, unrealistic and narcissistic, it can (as other writers have suggested) have damaging effects.

The nature of the Shaping Ego explains why this is the case. This is an ego prone to self-inflation. At a moderate level, this generates a confidence (perhaps unrealistic) that solutions can be found to current problems. At a more extreme level, it can produce a will to dominate and to absolve yourself of responsibility and blame. Shapers have received unconditional feedback from the 'mirrors' around them, and the reflections have always been somewhat distorted, sometimes badly so. The feedback can be subjective and solipsistic, unrelated to any actual, external evaluations. As Shapers grow up, however, they remain

---

[8] R F Baumeister, L Smart and J M Boden, 'Relation of Threatened Egotism to Violence and Aggression: the Dark Side of High Self-Esteem', *Psychological Review*, 103, pp5–33

convinced of their own likeableness and reject any contrary feedback. In one sense, they retain the kind of childlike view of self that all of us have sometimes known—that of the infallible superhero. By and large, children do not have an accurate view of themselves.

Tony Blair is an example of this. Over the years, he has given the impression of being resistant to criticism, and of being able to convince himself of his own rightness. He seems to have an unquestioning self-regard that basically dismisses the feedback he receives from outside. He trusts himself—he also trusts others—and fails to see why people should not endlessly trust him. It is this that has given him his eternal self-assurance, so attractive at first, as well as his independence of mind on issues such as Iraq.

The Shaping Ego pattern can produce tremendous qualities, as we have seen; but at its most extreme, when morally unconstrained, it can also show itself in terrible abuses. I suspect that Ronnie and Reggie Kray, the notorious London gangsters of the 1960s, were Shapers. Brought up in a strongly matriarchal home in the East End, they were devoted to their mother and she to them. She could never see anything bad in her angels, and she never required them to be responsible or properly self-critical or to think of others. In time, the twins created an extended 'safe family', but it became clear that they would do unspeakable harm to anyone who hurt their mother in any way. Their grandiose egos created a world that made sense on their terms, according to their ethics; and neither they nor their mother ever saw beyond it. They were what psychologists would call 'sociopaths': utterly committed to their own point of view and totally indifferent to anyone else's.

The Shaping Ego and leadership

How, then, do Shapers lead? What impact does their high level of trust, in themselves and in others, have on the way they lead people and on the culture they create around themselves?

Optimism

Shapers tend to be positive about what can be achieved. Where others see threats, they see opportunities. Optimism is a tremendously powerful quality—in a crisis, it is the very oxygen you need to survive. The story of Sir Ernest Shackleton, the British Antarctic explorer, illustrates the power of undiminished optimism in the face of the severest adversity. His 1914 expedition to the Antarctic in the *Endeavour* ground to a halt in an unbreakable ice-sheet, leaving the entire party stranded hundreds of miles from Elephant Island, the nearest land. Vowing that not one life would be lost, Shackleton inspired extraordinary loyalty and comradeship in his exhausted, frostbitten men, demanding that each of them believe in his capacity to see them safe. On 30 August 1916, more than four months after he had left them to go on an 800-mile, near-suicidal voyage to reach the nearest whaling station, Shackleton returned to rescue every single one.

Paternalism

Shapers tend to want to rescue people. This may be what is needed in Antarctic exploration, but for the long-term development of healthy adult followers it is, perhaps, less desirable. Outside of moments of crisis, it is often necessary for a leader to stay with his followers in their pain rather than simply sort out their problems for them. Dependence is a close cousin of paternalism.

Self-defined reality

Shapers tend to define their own reality. This gives them their ability to survive in tough situations that would overwhelm others: they simply do not experience those situations in the same way. Of all people, as leaders they need least approval or encouragement from others around them, and this can make them free in their choices—witness Blair's independence of mind on Iraq. Shapers do things their own way and believe that others should simply join them. This gives them the capacity for both the greatest service to and the greatest abuse of others. Often, they will work for a greater good when few others will; but they can also take their followers down a road that leads to nothing but their own personal vision.

It also gives them their tendency to unrealism. 'Power tends to corrupts, and absolute power corrupts absolutely.' Lying behind Lord Acton's observation is the Shaper, whose moral compass never points to quite the same north as everyone else's. Most of us align our behaviour to the norms of our wider society; but if my sensitivity to those norms is weak, because I define my own world, then normal social restraints will constrain my behaviour less. A warped morality (or even amorality) may result—and when that encounters political or military opportunity the results can be catastrophic. Dictators from Hitler to Mao have lacked the socializing norms that commonly restrain people.

Frontstage Shapers

The impression a frontstage Shaper gives is of self-assurance, even swagger. The audience watches with a mixture of admiration and awe as the leader rises to the challenges that lie ahead with supreme confidence. His regime smells of power, and in the face of his dominance the pretenders find other corners in which to exert their subordinate influence. There is often something pheromonal about frontstage Shapers when they get into leadership, something basic, biological and territorial. The options they offer are: compete or go elsewhere. The classic gun-slinging persona of Clint Eastwood, lounging through town, draws on the almost visceral appeal of the dominant frontstage Shaper. (Of course, the role can be played by women as well as men. The other most influential person in town could well be the madam of the local brothel, exercising a different but maybe equally exciting mix of power and seduction.) We are drawn to Eastwood's character: we want to be rescued by this mysterious and potent hero.

It's interesting to note how the world of the frontstage Shaper is either very safe or very unsafe. It is very safe if you are 'on his side'—protection is yours. However, for those on the back stage, in the shadows, life is very unsafe. The reality is that, while the Shaper exhibits a high level of trust in both himself and others on his front stage, backstage the opposite is true. There, his world is characterized by defensiveness and suspicion. It seems that, for a Shaper, once someone falls out of favour and is no longer seen as safe, they become a source of fear. Although the Shaper experiences most of the world as very safe, he experiences a part of it as very threatening.

Backstage Shapers

Nowhere is this more evident than in Mafia culture. The concept of 'cosa nostra' is classic backstage Shaping culture imprinted on family tradition, psychology and social consciousness. *Cosa nostra*—literally 'our thing'—expresses loyalty and commitment to your own community. To be inside 'the family' is to be safe, utterly safe. You will be protected, provided for, nurtured—a dependant of the 'family' which defines your reality. Within the 'family', morality is entirely self-referential: any action is justified to protect its interests and there is no need to take note of the rules of the world outside. Perhaps in organizations such as Enron and Arthur Andersen similar cultures evolved over time.

Cosa nostra is backstage Shaping culture where the only thing that matters is that you belong. In this culture, the world is divided between those who are trusted and those who are not. Those on the outside—in this case, on the front stage—are the dangerous ones. Mafia culture revolves around managing a world of suspicion and fear. It works because it creates a terrifying world for those on the front stage, outside the 'family'—they must either face being permanently under threat or find some way of 'buying into' the values (and favour) of those backstage. Membership of the 'family' promises safety; but for those members who jeopardize the 'family', by disloyalty or indiscretion, no punishment is too severe.

Many organizations, institutions and communities exhibit the influence of a Shaping Ego at the top. These are not necessarily hostile places; indeed, they are probably warm, comfortable places for which their members feel a great deal of affection. The insider's experience is of security, and probably also of privilege leading to loyalty. Often, the members of such a community are devoted, willing to make sacrifices and put up with privations for the sake of the family or firm. For many of us, this is very appealing. We crave the sense of belonging, as well as the perks. Businesses that cultivate talk of 'family' encourage just such an emotional attachment. And, of course, organizations such as the Freemasons have traded on such human needs for centuries.

Much about this culture is good and healing. But as leaders we must never forget that the seeds of paternalism and dependence are also sown in this kind of culture, and here, too, lie the roots of cold rejection. Whether they grow into full flower depends on the sensitivity of the leader, as well as the supporting scaffolds she places around her.

Study questions 7

1. What childhood influences form a Shaping Ego?
2. What characteristics does a Shaping Ego display in terms of
   · behaviours?
   · attitudes to others?
   · attitudes to themself?
3. What leadership characteristics tend to be seen in a Shaper?
4. How is the Shaping Ego expressed on
   · the front stage?
   · the back stage?
5. Who have you experienced as a Shaping leader? What was their impact on their followers
   · positively?
   · negatively?

EIGHT

Our Response to Trust: The Defining Leadership Ego—Drivenness and Ambition

What marks out the person with the Shaping Ego is their general feeling of security. The other three egos have one, opposite characteristic in common: to them, the world can never be unconditionally safe—and for the Defining Ego it is predominantly a critical and judgemental place.

Imagine a child growing up in a home where expectations about behaviour are very clear. For example, her parents may encourage good behaviour through some system of rewards and sanctions—a 'star chart' perhaps, or a pocket-money scheme. They may try to model good behaviour to their child, seeing it as their role to exemplify the kind of life she should aspire to. They may shower praise on her when she does well at school and take an enthusiastic interest in any good news she brings home. They may teach her to make sound and sensible judgements thoughout her life. In such ways, a moral curriculum is pursued, in which certain values are taught by them and 'caught' by her. In Bowlby's terms, the attachments are strong, but conditional.

Imagine the child's ego forming in such an environment. Little by little, she may interpret the 'sense-making' system of her parents and learn how to flourish within it. She may understand that, as long as she stays within the boundaries, she will generally receive plenty of approval and affirmation. She may find that it pays to do things that are within the canon of worthy and good behaviours, because that is how to get attention. She may also discover, to her cost, the sense of dismay when she falls short. No doubt many such children are spared full-on condemnation, but those that are sensitive may still pick up the unspoken disappointment.

What happens in the landscape of the ego is that the child starts to 'seed' the plants that will win favour. It may be a matter of achievement at school, or the development of a talent, or displays of such qualities as kindness or drive. The landscape is soon well defined by a string of successes, which have been received with delight and praise. Achievement in itself is reduced to a Pavlovian stimulus, providing the cue for X—her caregivers—to give approval. The child learns to provide the cue in order to get the approval. Increasingly, she also learns to avoid activities that might lead to disapproval. Thus, her landscape begins to tell a tale of both successes achieved and failures averted. Indeed, as she develops her own self-concept, the potential critic ceases to be her parents, or her teacher or youth-group leader, and becomes her herself. She is increasingly self-critical, evaluating what she does by her own, internal standards.

The child learns that it is always best to win. Losing is something to avoid because when she loses, the approval is (or she expects it to be) withdrawn. She learns that it is up to her whether she gains approval: she has the power in herself to get it—or not. She learns to trust herself, but not trust others. Other people, she predicts, will always look at her conditionally, will always score her and rank her. Approval will be withdrawn if she does not demonstrate competence in every field. She learns to weed out of her life anything she isn't good at. Life becomes highly selective, a matter of avoiding situations in which she might fail. She comes to think of herself as competent, but always under pressure. She is only as good as her last win.

What emerges from this is a high level of trust in herself but little trust in others. Her trust of self is high because, by and large, her life has been a catalogue of achievement of the targets she has set. There is a positive story to tell here that probably involves individual discipline and sacrifice. While other children have been larking around, rebelling or just drifting through their teenage years, the Defining Ego has been training herself to live up to the required standard. Her trust in others is low, however, because the fear lurks that, if for some reason she was unable to maintain the standard she has set, criticism and condemnation would follow. Her expectation is that others will judge her on the basis of her performance, not of who she is.

Somehow, all her cumulative achievement means nothing to her: it is as if she keeps on winning trophies but each new one is an illusion, because each one merely gives her the message that she has met the standard this time. She is trapped by the sense that she can always fail next time and must therefore drive herself on, avoiding failure, avoiding letting herself down. Whereas once she achieved in order to secure the approval of X, now it has become an internal imperative simply to sustain her sense of self, regardless of who is watching. She is driven by insatiable inner standards that can never really be attained. Each day, she is set another target and feels she has to hit it. She is defined by what she achieves, and afraid of what she can't.

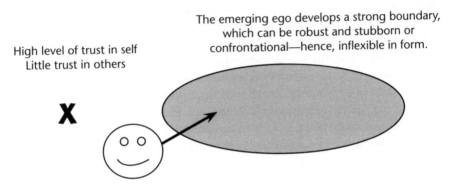

The emerging ego develops a strong boundary, which can be robust and stubborn or confrontational—hence, inflexible in form.

High level of trust in self
Little trust in others

X

X perceived as conditional

Diagram 8.1   The pattern of the Defining Ego

It doesn't take a highly judgemental home for a child to develop such an ego. Merely the good intentions of a caring and educative environment can be enough. Of course, most parents want to be encouraging, praising the positive, and it is often only a short step to become parents who give out subtle signals of disappointment when the standard is not met. There are many educational and nurturing institutions that are set up to give the same kinds of feedback: do well and you get rewarded, fail and there are consequences. Schools promote achievement with all kinds of status and status symbols, creating a hierarchy of those who are successful and those who are not. 'Doing well' is a way to secure power, prestige and reputation.

Some children are particularly sensitive to the praise of adults and fear letting them down. Indeed, sometimes the most loving and affirming homes can foster an over-conscientious desire on the part of children to live up to their parents' expectations and dreams. Nasser Hussein was captain of the England cricket team between 1999 and 2003. As a child, he had been intense and, as his talent began to emerge, he was aware that his father took pride in him as a promising sportsman. Those early years of strong parental approval of a gift he worked hard to cultivate established an ego whose standards Hussein had to measure up to throughout his professional career. He described how, as captain of England, he would dread the prospect of batting, the very thing he excelled at. The night before he was due to bat, he would sleep fitfully, waking up to rehearse strokes in his mind. He could hardly bear to go to sleep again, for fear of hastening the time when he would have to walk out to the crease. Instead, he would count the minutes, allowing himself to fend off the fear of his forthcoming ordeal for as long as possible.

For Hussein, what had started as a delightful gift that he enjoyed became a terrible threat that robbed him of joy and filled him with fear at the prospect of failure. However good his last innings had been, however many centuries he had scored to date, each time he went to the crease it was to have his worth as a batsman—indeed, his whole life—scrutinized and possibly trashed. Failure would mean not merely a bad innings to get over but the dismissal of his gift, perhaps even of his identity. Faced with such a prospect, it is no wonder that he found the anxiety so exhausting. In the end, Hussein resigned the captaincy and a burden visibly lifted from his shoulders. The following year, he retired altogether from first-class cricket, only three days after scoring a match-winning century against New Zealand.

The Defining Ego can be understood as a house of cards. In terms of achievement and accomplishment, the standards set and the discipline and sacrifice required to meet them, it is impressive indeed. You may marvel at what has been attempted and attained: others would have given up, or would never have aimed so high. The Defining Ego flatters itself by its commitment to live up to its own self-expectations. However, like a house of cards, the edifice is precarious. If the next card falls, it will send the whole thing crashing to the ground. The reason for this is easy to appreciate: others cannot be trusted to give unconditional acceptance, and you expect them to be judgemental. You have prevented their criticism by perpetual success, but if once you fail, your whole life will be evaluated and found wanting. The one thing the Definer has 'bought' with his avoidance of failure is avoidance of rejection. To experience failure is, in his mind, to face rejection, and that is the one thing he is most afraid of. However, like a high jumper who has to set the bar higher and higher, the Definer is condemned to fail in the end. One day, the bar will simply be too high. And when it is, the prospect that faces him will be the rejection he fears, or even self-annihilation.

The Defining Ego and leadership

How, then, do Definers lead? What impact do this high level of trust in themselves and little trust in others have on the way they lead people and on the culture they create around themselves?

Performance, not success

Definers will create around them a culture driven by the pursuit of better performance. This may be in terms of quality, productivity, sales, costs or efficiency, depending on their field of operation. However, improving performance is not the same as achieving success. Success, as something to be enjoyed and celebrated, is not experienced. What is achieved is the avoidance of failure. Current victories are soon left behind, 'good but not as good as they could be'. If 9 out of 10 is attained, the focus will be on why it wasn't 10. If 19 positive things are said in the feedback, the focus will be on the one negative. The joy of success is chilled by the spectre of failure, preventing celebration and inner peace, creating an incessant demand for more or better that can never be satisfied.

In the television series *The Apprentice*, Alan Sugar (or, in the American original, Donald Trump) puts a group of 14 potential employees through a series of business challenges in what amounts to a 12-week job interview. One by one, they are weeded out in a culture that epitomizes the leadership of the Defining Ego. Only one thing matters: performance. Nothing is ever as good as it could be, and even the best performances are criticized rather than celebrated. The entire project is fuelled by fear—you can almost smell the adrenalin. Such is the corporate world today, very often, where success consists in seeing your rival go under, and you are only as good as your last deal.

Control and lack of delegation

In an environment of fear, control is everything. To lose control is to risk error and therefore failure. The Defining Ego inevitably and relentlessly moves away from diversity and spontaneity towards conformity and homogeneity. Systems become increasingly sophisticated and complex in an effort to reduce the threat of disorder. Delegation becomes little more than instrumental execution of the operational orders. Freedom to trust yourself and think for yourself is sacrificed on the altar of control.

The England rugby union team won the World Cup in 2003 on a Defining regime. The fact of the matter was that they were better prepared, had spent more money, had left less to chance and followed a tighter game plan than any other team. Their head coach, Clive Woodward, was ruthless in dumping established members of the team if they lost form. His favourite comment after a game, whether they had won or lost, was 'We move on, we move on.' However, while the strategy served the team well for a time, it hit the rocks soon after, when many of the same players returned to New Zealand with the same head coach to play for the British and Irish Lions. By then, the All Blacks had learned Woodward's game plan and adapted. None of the Lions thought for themselves or trusted their own judgement on the field. They looked like automata playing out a pre-programmed set of moves, without the flexibility or the confidence in their own and each other's ability to adapt to a fluid game. Paralysed by fear of 'getting it wrong', the legacy of the Defining Ego culture is a lack of freedom to take risks. The Lions lost the series 0-3 and conceded more points than ever before in the process.

Avoiding risk

Taking risks involves freedom to fail. Once failure has been identified as the arch-enemy, the possibility of taking risks diminishes. A few years back, I did some work for a large multinational pharmaceutical company. It coincided with an ambiguous set of results from its clinical trials for a new 'wonder' drug for lung cancer. The value of the company's shares plummeted as investors reacted to the news. What was interesting was what happened to the culture of this company. Previously known for its willingness to innovate in staff welfare as well as drug development, it changed its emphasis to systems controls. It tightened up the way supplies and services were ordered and managed, abandoned drug-development programmes which didn't have an almost cast-iron guarantee of success and concentrated on exploiting the markets for existing, already proven drugs.

The current shareholder-capital system of our publicly quoted companies is, in essence, a Defining culture. All that matters is performance: you are only as good as your last deal (or, in this case, drug). To thrive in such an environment as a leader, you would need yourself to be totally performance-focused, for the system doesn't tolerate failure.

Frontstage Definers

Definers are often the highest achievers, able to marshal considerable personal resources of discipline, focus and self-belief. Many of the world's most extraordinary achievements—in mathematics, art, engineering, medicine, science, exploration and war—would have been possible only through the drive of often a single Defining Ego. However, in order to sustain their sense of self, Definers invest huge amounts of energy in working hard, and very often they become driven or full of anxiety, never able to relax. This may lead them in one of two directions. The first is to avoid going onto their back stage. They spend their energy achieving on their front stage, amassing the trophies and the acolytes they need around them to reassure themselves of their potency; but they rarely spend any time backstage, because to do that would require taking their eye off their frontstage performance. They may come to deplore self-reflection, which they see as negative. Sadly, they may neglect their personal and emotional lives, allowing personal relationships to decay. They are sometimes willing to sacrifice all manner of values backstage in order to sustain what is going on out front.

Then, of course, the day may come when they crash. They lose their job, or their spouse announces that they have had enough of years of neglect, or their grown-up son or daughter says they don't want to know them—and who are they anyway? Then, amidst the pain, they realize what it has cost them to maintain that frontstage performance, and truth may come bearing down on them like a tidal wave. Tragically, things are too far gone for some Definers for them to recover. Relationships may be lost irrevocably. For some it may be too late to develop any kind of personal and emotional language even to begin to address all the hurts and deficits there are. They may now simply be ill equipped to make that kind of journey. All that is left to them is to try and hold onto the fragments. Some remain broken, others turn sadly back to their careers and become even more driven and ruthless than before, denying those around them the freedom to do what they have denied themselves. As leaders, they tend to become territorial, defending their status from everyone they perceive as a threat. Every situation is seen as a win-lose situation. Losing becomes even more fearful, failure is not tolerated, poor performance is eliminated.

They may begin to develop a culture of 'deliver or be delivered from the company'. Often, the success of the firm becomes *their* success, and they resist any attempts to be dislodged from their position. In the end, they may go into retirement, probably with a sense of fear in their guts, having lost most of their relationships, consigned to a one-dimensional life, picking over the bones of the good things they have allowed to rot around them. Big cars and golfing holidays are scant consolation for their restless loneliness. Moreover, they tend to age gracelessly, raging against their diminishing faculties, never having learned how to trust others and receive as they have to let go of their beloved control and autonomy and power. They have the indignity of having to allow others to serve them and clean them. They discover their mortality but they face their demise ill prepared, finding that all the scripts and performances they have delivered were on the wrong stage. On the back stage, which is all that really matters now, they have little on which to draw.

Such a bleak prognosis need not be the case, however. For those who are willing to humble themselves, seek forgiveness from those they have hurt and try to learn again what it means to be human, redemption and even restoration are possible. Hope still remains.

Backstage Definers

The second direction the Defining Ego can go in in leadership is away from their front stage towards their back stage. They begin to find that the safest way to sustain the high standards they expect of themselves is to hide them away backstage, behind the curtain. There are several advantages in doing this. First, it means that if they fail, they fail privately. Public failure is what they really fear, but if they keep their standards secret—nursing them late into the night, in their hearts where no one else can see—only they will know whether they have succeeded or failed. This way, if they do fall short they can usually find a way of 'rescripting' it. 'It wasn't a failure, it was a learning opportunity. The pass mark was unachievable. The examiners were wrong. I could have done better if I'd really put everything into it, but I chose to hold back. My best is still to come!'

They become experts at avoiding defeat and sustaining their sense that they really have lived up to their own standards by embracing little fantasies and self-delusions. Meanwhile, they eliminate from their lives all the things they can't succeed in. They avoid any risk and start using aphorisms such as 'If a job's worth doing, it's worth doing well!' They become 'all or nothing' people, committing themselves only to those things in which they can win. They exhibit a strange mixture of passion and commitment on some occasions and passive detachment, apathy or depression on others, when they see no point in trying at all.

These backstage Definers have learned that no one likes a bighead, so they keep their achievements to themselves. They are known as modest, self-deprecating and understated, qualities that are all the more appealing because of their obvious gifts and skills. They choose to present a compliant face to the world. However, locked in their private world of secret goals and visions, they risk falling into fantasy and solipsism. Many feel frustrated on a daily basis that they aren't able to turn their dreams into reality. Many feel endlessly disappointed that they cannot be publicly who they privately think themselves to be. Many live in a lonely world in which they just accept that no one will ever know who they really are.

Some develop an anxiety syndrome to do with control, or Obsessive-Compulsive Disorder as an external mechanism to establish control of things that in themselves they cannot resolve. Others develop a depression, a mental cage into which they retreat and lock themselves away. In there it may be dark, it may be grey, but at least it can be safe. When you're depressed, you can let yourself off the hook—nothing can be expected of you. Depression is a mechanism many Definers adopt unconsciously as the only way to loosen the chains of self-imposed expectations that bind them every day. And in that depression they may nurse a fatalistic belief that the world will never be any different and they are consigned to live in their private world, alone. There is no point to anything.

As leaders, backstage Definers often fluctuate between being passionate and being apathetic, being committed and being world-weary and cynical, being involved and being withdrawn. Deep down, they long for the freedom that 'being found and accepted for who they are' would bring. Tragically, some never find such honesty and safety. However, others do make the difficult journey out of that lonely place. It is wonderful how the intimate support of a faithful, loving relationship can foster confidence in a defended soul and encourage them to climb into light and freedom.

Of course, the pictures I have painted here are extreme, caricatures designed to draw attention to the most dramatic of behaviours. Many readers will relate in small ways to milder versions of these attitudes at times in their life. It is helpful for all of us to be aware of our own pathologies, however moderate they may seem to be.

Study questions 8

1. What childhood influences form a Defining Ego?
2. What characteristics does a Defining Ego display in terms of
   - behaviours?
   - attitudes to others?
   - attitudes to themself?
3. What leadership characteristics tend to be seen in a Defining leader?
4. How is the Defining Ego expressed on
   - the front stage?
   - the back stage?
5. Who have you experienced as a Defining leader? What was their impact on their followers
   - positively?
   - negatively?

NINE

Our Response to Trust: The Adapting Leadership Ego—Anxiety and Over-Responsibility

The one thing the Shaping Ego and the Defining Ego have in common is a high level of trust in themselves. For different reasons, both back themselves and expect to succeed. The third ego doesn't share this presumption. The Adapter has little trust in themself, but a high level of trust in others.

Imagine a child growing up in an environment in which he sees his relationship with his caregivers, X, as fragile—or, in Bowlby's terms, insecure. In other words, his perception is that the rope may easily break. There may be several reasons for this, and it is worth looking at each in turn.

In one home, X is remote or even absent. Dad is preoccupied with work and has little time or attention to give to the child; Mum is detached and withdrawn as a result of things she is struggling with in her own life. Maybe they are busy with the emotional needs of his many other siblings and so there is little adult attention to go round. In such circumstances, the child must develop a coping mechanism. One such may be to try to secure a parent's attention in some way. He may develop a funny routine—he's discovered that when he does such-and-such, other people watch and laugh. Or he may make himself useful, finding ways to help out around the home. He cultivates his 'performance' because it clearly 'works'—it attracts and holds the audience's attention for a few minutes, which is what he needs. In fact, he sees other people much as an uncertain stage-performer may see their audience. People may lose interest at any time, there are many other shows they could go and watch. What the performer has to do is to master techniques that secure their continuing interest and attention. What both performer and child are trying to achieve is to prevent the fragile relationship breaking so that they are rejected. They sense that unless they continue to secure it, this is what may happen.

In another home, a child experiences the significant adults around them as emotionally 'full'. People become like this when they are unable to deal with all the emotions inside them. This could be the case if a parent is sad or depressed, perhaps having suffered a loss or bereavement. The child may sense that she can't 'risk' expressing any of her own feelings or needs because that would 'break' the adult, who is not robust enough to contain it. This could also be the case if a parent is full of unresolved anger. The child experiences them as volatile and so can't take the risk of doing anything to 'set the explosion off'. Psychologists recognize that in order for a person to express their own emotional needs, they need to feel that they will be heard and 'held'—in other words, that there is a space for their own needs to be contained. Many of us will recognize this ourselves. Think for a moment of the person you would go to talk to if you were anxious or depressed. There are probably lots of people who instantly come to mind who, despite being good friends or even family, you *wouldn't* want to go to. The person you would choose is the one who will listen without judging or condemning you, who will accept you and 'hold' your emotions without making you argue them away or bottle them up again. What we want and need is a container into which to pour out our own emotional mess and for it to be held by someone else. We need the relationship to be 'big and strong enough' to cope with that.

There is another situation that, ironically, creates a sense of fragility, and that is when conflict and confrontation are not appropriately modelled in the home. Many leaders I deal with talk about how loving and peaceful their childhood home was. Press them a little further and you discover that theirs was a home in which no one ever got angry, conflict was not done, issues were buried. They never saw Mum or Dad lose their temper, shout or yell. Everything was quiet and, apparently, happy. The consequence of this apparent idyll is that the child never discovers whether his relationship with X is strong enough to survive a conflict. It is as if he were growing up not knowing whether the ropes around him are strong or weak. He is terrified that they will break, because he has no experience of ropes coping with a good 'tug of war', or being repaired when they become frayed. The child internalizes the idea that, because the ropes have never been tested, they may be fragile; and he predicts that it would be devastating if they broke, because he has never experienced this happening. And he will do anything to avoid it happening. The irony of an apparently secure home in which arguments never have to be resolved because they never take place is that it can produce not a secure child but one who grows up to be insecure.

In all three of these situations, an ego can form that has little trust in itself but a high level of trust in others. The child does all he can to prevent the relationship breaking.

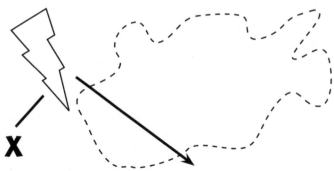

Little trust in self
High level of trust in others

The emerging ego develops only a weak boundary, which remains open but is extremely flexible and accommodating.

The relation with X perceived as fragile

Diagram 9.1   The pattern of the Adapting Ego

Frontstage Adapters

This pattern can work itself out in one of two ways. First, on the front stage, the child develops an attention-seeking performance and maintains this strategy into her adult life. In any group, there is usually someone who needs to have the attention on them all or most of the time. Often, they are the first to speak in a discussion. Often, they find a question to ask the group leader, and have their hand up first in a lecture. They seem to need to have other people's eyes upon them. The reality is that they 'know who they are' when they have other people's attention—and they don't when that attention turns elsewhere. The borders of their ego 'landscape' are wide open and they invite people to come in and approve of what they find inside. Because of this, they tend to seek out exciting situations where there is plenty of warmth and optimism about. They need to feel part of something that gives them worth and purpose.

Many of the characters played by Woody Allen suffer from this kind of extreme neurosis about their social relationships. Insecure about their looks, worried about the impression they are making, they try to be helpful but often end up being a nuisance instead. Perhaps the character played by Ben Stiller in the recent film *Meet the Fockers* sends up such an ego best. Stiller plays the son-in-law attempting to ingratiate himself in the ruthlessly Defining culture of his fiancée's family. He is up against Robert de Niro's father-in-law, a former CIA agent who is the epitome of distrust of others. Every attempt Stiller makes to be useful and pleasant of course only adds to the disaster, culminating in him burning down the whole wedding reception. Such social neurosis is easy to send up, but a lower level of it is prevalent in much of the population—which is, of course, why we laugh at it: we can see enough of ourselves to feel the pain!

Then, there is often the Adapter person who is the team 'glue'. This is the person who goes around ensuring that everyone is doing OK. They sense when people are being excluded or overlooked and will go and make sure they are all right. They detect disagreement and will find ways to placate people and play down differences in order to smooth over any conflict in the group. They secure the affection of others around them by being caring, supportive and positive, drawing attention to others rather than themselves. The thing they fear is being left out of the group, so they stop the group leaving people out.

Finally, there are the problem solvers in the group, the ones who cannot be without something to contribute. They are the ones who are always coming up with a better way to do things—indeed, even if it works fine just as it is they seem to manufacture a problem so they can fix it. If they can make a drama out of a crisis, they will. Indeed, the real problem for them is when there is no problem, because having something to fix is what assures them of their worth and secures the relationships they feel are fragile. It is no surprise that often these people end up in the caring professions, working in contexts where everyone is in need and they can be reassured every day that their need, and the relationships with those around them, will not be taken away.

At its best, this kind of behaviour can create warmth and care for those around. Many voluntary organizations are staffed by Adapters sacrificially giving their time, skill and energy to make a difference. However, the darker side of this character is what I sometimes refer to as 'emotional incontinence': an inability to control appropriately the effluence of your emotion, and a need to seek reassurance all the time from those around you. 'High-maintenance people' is another term we sometimes use to describe such people. In effect, they co-opt others around them into 'maintaining' them by containing their emotion for them. Like leaky sieves, their feelings and responses simply pour out of them. The answer, of course, is for the sieve to become a pan and develop the capacity and responsibility to contain emotion itself. For the frontstage Adapter, this feels very risky, because emotion is the principal currency with which they purchase attention and affection. To contain it would be to reduce their buying power.

Backstage Adapters

The second way the Adapting Ego can work itself out is on the back stage. If frontstage Adapting can sometimes end up as emotional incontinence, backstage adapting can be thought of as emotional containment. This occurs when someone habitually bottles up their feelings rather than taking the risk of expressing them. The trigger for them will have been the sense that it is just too dangerous to express your own feelings. Millions of people habitually 'self-hold' (the psychological term to describe the mechanism by which a person retains their own emotions within themselves rather than allowing them to be dealt with by others). When a person does this, they manage to preserve a fragile relationship from breaking by not putting any undue stress on it. Rather than expressing their own needs, or articulating their anger, or asking for help, they bottle it up. They internalize blame and guilt and idealize others around them, absolving others of responsibility for their actions—even, at times, the cruellest and grossest actions.

Over time, of course, this produces a deficit of affection and self-love: crushed self-esteem. Years of suppressing your own needs and serving other people's leaves a legacy of anxiety, guilt, resentment or self-loathing as well as exhaustion. At its most extreme, this is the kind of ego that will allow itself to be used and abused. Ironically, and tragically, the self-destruction involved in an abusive relationship can become the very thing such a person believes they must experience.

This kind of person tends, as they grow into adulthood, to become compliant and adaptive, finding ways of fitting in and repressing their own needs. They will often allow others to win rather than them; and, in order to protect their perception of someone else, will appropriate blame that is not properly theirs. Their opinion of themselves becomes too low as they continually put themselves in situations where they allow others to win by letting themselves lose. They seek to serve others and say 'yes' to them. They find saying 'no' to people very difficult, because unconsciously they fear that, if they do, the relationship may well break down. They become people with an overdeveloped sense of duty, conscientiousness and commitment.

In Steven Spielberg's war film *Saving Private Ryan*, the Rangers captain played by Tom Hanks is sent with his platoon to rescue Private James Ryan from the front line. All of Ryan's brothers have been killed in combat and American military policy demanded that the last remaining son should be brought home. In the event, the rescue costs the lives of many men and the scene of battle ends poignantly with Hanks's captain gasping his dying words to the young private: 'Earn it! Earn it!'

Ryan gets out alive, and we see him finally as an old man, visiting a cemetery in France some 50 years later with his family to pay his respects at the graves of the men who died to bring him home. 'Tell me I have been a good man,' he begs his wife, in tears. 'Tell me I have been a good man!' The rest of his life had been almost a penance for the price that was paid to save him. He bore on his shoulders the weight of the captain's exhortation, the duty that had to be fulfilled, the perpetual guilt that his life should have been saved while others were lost. Such is the moral and emotional burden of the Adapter.

Such is the emotional appeal made by some Christian teaching in the church. In this case, it is not a platoon of soldiers sent to save a life but Jesus, the man Christians believe to be the Son of God. In accomplishing his rescue mission, Jesus willingly laid down his life—indeed, Christians believe that this act of self-sacrifice is central to how we can obtain forgiveness and be reconciled with God. In response to such sacrifice, the writers in the New Testament encourage followers of Jesus to 'live a life worthy of the Lord'. There is, of course, a right and healthy sense of thankfulness and love to someone who has given his life to save yours. However, unless you are careful, being a Christian can become a daily penance, an observance of a duty of gratitude, burdened by a perpetual feeling of guilt for what was done for you. When the death of Jesus is understood in this way, the gospel of life becomes just another kind of slavery.

The Adapting Ego and leadership

How, then, do Adapters lead?

Following, not leading

For the Adapter, leadership is a daily battle. Once again, things can go one of two ways. On the one hand, the leader may seek to do his adapting on the front stage of the organization—usually, with regard to the relationships around him. For him, leadership involves popularity, approval and attention. Consequently, Adapters lead by 'licking their fingers and sticking them into the wind,' as Jim Wallis says of politicians.[9]

In fact, they follow rather than lead. They find ways of ingratiating themselves, of staying in, of keeping people on board. This may mean that they get into patterns of playing off one group against another or of telling half-truths rather than the whole, uncomfortable truth. They rarely confront bullies properly or resolve conflict by dealing with the issues. Usually, they look for a way to paper over the cracks rather than finding the courage to try to repair the widening fissure. Of course they work very hard—too hard—giving every hour of the day to justify their existence and demonstrate their worth.

Denial, not freedom

On the other hand, the Adapter in leadership may go backstage. When this happens, he keeps his insecure, adaptive self well hidden. Instead, he presents a persona that is excessively confident and in control, which is designed to mask his insecurities and deny his need for love and affection. So determined are they that no one will ever find out quite how insecure they feel behind the curtain that they put on a bravura performance, saying all the right things, talking the talk. Driven by their sense of obligation, they push themselves harder and harder, getting exhausted, wrung out, while the organization takes more and more. In the end, they find they are trapped: they cannot give any less at work, but how can they ever own up to what is going on behind the mask? How can they be honest? How can they be real? Will anyone ever know the real them? They long to be known, and accepted for who they are; and yet they can't take the risk of letting anyone see—in case they see what they're really like and walk away.

Meanwhile, the duty they offer increasingly has strings attached. They serve (unconsciously) in order to get some return. They hope for thanks and approval and if they don't get them they feel resentful. They deny themselves to serve others, but envy those who are preferred over them. Their own unmet emotional deficit starts to leak out. It may come out in angry outbursts and

---

[9] Wallis, *Faith Works*, p173

irrational decisions. It may come out in anxiety and panic. It may express itself in physical ways, in stress-related illnesses, irritable bowel syndrome or high blood pressure. The pressure the Adapter puts themself under will find a way to escape, whether managed or unmanaged. The long-term legacy will probably be ill health of one form or another, resulting in loss of productivity or performance—the very thing they despise in themselves.

Giving, not receiving

Adapters are almost certainly the hardest workers in an organization, working longer hours and going the extra mile. Giving to others is the thing that gives them their sense of identity. In the Bible, there is a story of two sisters, Mary and Martha, who Jesus visited one day as their friend. Martha busied herself preparing a meal for their guest, while Mary sat at Jesus' feet listening to him. In the end, Martha's frustration boiled over. 'Lord, don't you care that my sister has left me to do the work by myself? Tell her to help me!' Expecting his support and some criticism of Mary's laziness, she was taken aback when Jesus replied, 'Martha, Martha, you are upset and worried about many things, but only one thing is needed. Mary has chosen what is better and it will not be taken away from her.'[10]

To her surprise, Martha was invited to discover that giving is not always better than receiving. Indeed, for the Adapting Ego receiving is far more of a challenge. It involves placing yourself in someone's debt and accepting with humility the service of another. It takes away your control and invites you to allow someone else to love you and have power over you.

In an organization, the ability to receive as a leader is a mark of trust and health. Leaders must first allow themselves to be led. Otherwise, they will end up leading people in order to satisfy their own unmet needs.

---

[10] Luke 10.38-42

Study questions 9

1. What childhood influences form an Adapting Ego?
2. What characteristics does an Adapting Ego display in terms of
   - behaviours?
   - attitudes to others?
   - attitudes to themself?
3. What leadership characteristics tend to be seen in an Adapting leader?
4. How is the Adapting Ego expressed on
   - the front stage?
   - the back stage?
5. Who have you experienced as an Adapting leader? What was their impact on their followers
   - positively?
   - negatively?

TEN

Our Response to Trust: The Defending Leadership Ego—Suspicion and Over-Sensitivity

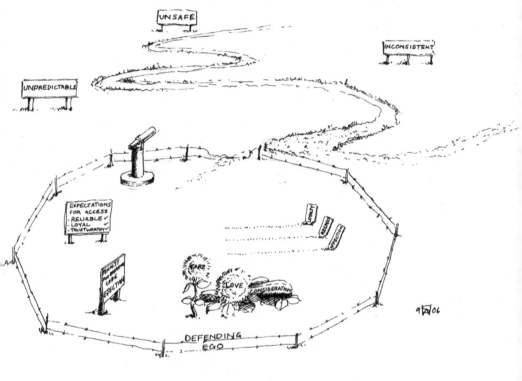

The fourth and last of the egos we need to explore is the one that has little trust either of self or of others: the Defending Ego.

Imagine a child who grows up in a relationship with X that she perceives as being unreliable (and it is important to note that we are talking about perception, which may or may not reflect reality). In Bowlby's terms, we would call this 'disorganized'. Let me tell you about Max. Max is five and lives with his nan, Paula, along with his brother, who is eight, and his sister, who is 11.

The reason they live with Paula is that both their parents are drug addicts. Max was born into a dangerous and dysfunctional home and Paula's generous and sacrificial care has been nothing short of a rescue. However, life for her is tough—very tough: she is in her sixties and has already brought up a family of her own as a single mother. She manages mainly on benefits, and yet will always spend lavishly on the children for birthdays and Christmas, running herself into debt.

Max's experience of home is of inconsistency. Sometimes, he is showered with love—spoiled, even. At other times, he is left in the unreliable care of his father, when his nan is just too exhausted to cope. If his father is not around, it may be his mother, who pops up out of the blue when she is not off her head. Or Max may be looked after by his uncle and his current girlfriend, who will (on past form) probably be around for a year or so. Max's experience of caregivers is unpredictable and chaotic. Sometimes it is secure, at other times it is precarious; sometimes he feels safe, at other times, he doesn't. He knows what to expect on some mornings, but on others he may not get breakfast or make it to school on time. It's hard for Max to grow up with any sense of stability, order and predictability about his attachments.

Max's situation may seem quite extreme, but there are many who experience far worse. It is not just the obviously dysfunctional families, however, that give their children unreliable care. A father who is volatile, aggressive or just bad-tempered and difficult to predict is an unreliable caregiver. So is a mother who suffers from some form of manic depression, or simply mood swings, who is intimate and affectionate one day but remote and closed in on herself the next. A family that uproots from one culture and moves to another, perhaps one with a different language, breaking up friendships and rocking the child's sense of place and routine; or a family in which Mum and Dad have split up and one of them is now an unpredictable presence, sometimes present, sometimes not—they, too, may give unreliable care. A child who is misunderstood at school from an early age and labelled as a troublemaker and untrustworthy, and therefore is treated with suspicion by people who should be on his side—he, too, experiences unreliable care.

In fact, disorganized and unreliable attachments are becoming ever more prevalent in our society as the family as an institution fractures, as peoples are displaced and migrate for work, as the proportion of parents on antidepressants or anxiety-related drugs increases. In Britain, it is estimated that the number of marriages that will end in divorce will soon reach nearly 50 per cent, and that one in every two people experiences a broken family, as a child or an adult. That is not to say that all who experience such things develop Defending strategies; but it is to say that for many children the world is unreliable and hard to predict—and adults are difficult to trust.

Faced with such a world, the child has to develop a strategy to cope, and one such strategy is a low trust of other people. Let me illustrate it this way. Imagine I am playing in an American football team and you are on my side. I'm a running back and you're a defensive linesman. Your job is to stop people 'hitting' me by blocking opponents and creating a pathway for me to run through. If you don't do that, I'm going to get whacked. Imagine now that I discover that sometimes you're reliable and on your game, but at other times you are simply not. Maybe you get distracted sometimes, or simply don't fancy taking the hits yourself. If that is the case, I can't rely on you to create holes for me to run through; I can't rely on you to protect me. I can't rely on you to be on my side. Now what do I do? Well, one thing I can do is to avoid running down the channel you should be protecting. Even though sometimes you put up a great block, it's not worth me taking the risk, so I simply opt out of trusting you. Another thing I can do is to become an expert at spotting whether you seem to be 'in the game'. If I can learn how to pick up your signals, when you are losing interest, or are distracted, or are not up for it, if I can tell whether you're about to let me down, then I can choose whether to run down your channel or not. It gives me some control and it gives me a measure of safety, in what would otherwise be a dangerous situation.

Now, a child is much the same. She will learn not to trust someone who is inconsistent and unreliable—it's just not worth the risk of getting let down or hurt, especially if it is their job to protect her. Remember that children are small people and face a big world: if their 'blocker' isn't on their side, they may well get hit by some heavy traffic coming the other way. They will come to distrust others around them, to be suspicious and cautious of placing themselves in another's care. Moreover, if they *do* trust someone and that person then lets them down, they will withdraw, no question. That will be it. For the child, the only way to make that dangerous situation safe is to pull back, to avoid the same thing happening again.

At the same time, this child may develop the skill to 'read' people to see if they're going to be on her side. She becomes good at interpreting expressions, tones of voice, body language. She knows when to get out of the way, to avoid the hit before it comes. She develops a number of defensive strategies to avoid being hurt or let down: she will probably be oversensitive when she is criticized, she may interpret people as being against her when they are not, she may personalize issues and blame people she feels are being disloyal. She will be good at seeing who is on her side and will cultivate those relationships to make her secure. She will value loyalty and be loyal herself—to those she does trust—as a means of securing the same commitment in return.

Pauline was someone who had been let down throughout her life—by her mum and her dad, her convent school and her tutors. When I met her, I quickly came to see that there were two kinds of people in Pauline's world: those who were safe and those who were not. The safe people were those who had never let her down. These, like her husband and other priests she had known, she adored and relied on—she would have done anything for them. She trusted every word they said and hung on them, sometimes with a misguided loyalty, I felt. The unsafe people were those who had let her down. On this list were her arch-enemies of old, but also recent friends who had not quite lived up to expectations.

Knowing Pauline was like joining a private members' club. At first, she was suspicious of you. You felt as if you were under inspection as she checked you out at a distance and evaluated you to see if you could be trusted. Then, when she felt sure enough that you were reliable, she began to let you in; and this gave you access to all kinds of benefits—she was generous and kind and affirming, your greatest supporter and ally. In this way, you came to enjoy membership of an intimate, special and (you were conscious) somewhat exclusive club.

At the same time, you were aware that you yourself could be blackballed at any time: if you let her down, if you didn't keep your word, if you went behind her back, if you dared to criticize her or were not entirely supportive of her opinions, you were out. The doors would be shut, the trust gone. I felt as if I was permanently on probation. I was proud that, unlike others, I was not on Pauline's blacklist; and I was anxious not to earn a place on it by being unreliable.

The Defending strategy is all about dividing the world up into the safe and the unsafe. People are seen as falling into one or other category—there is nothing in between. The world to a Defender is a dangerous place, from which you have to protect yourself. To do that, you have to become cautious, suspicious and fiercely loyal to those you have admitted into your personal life. I have known many Defenders. Steve was a football coach who regarded me as his greatest ally through the season when I was 'on his side', but after I questioned a decision I was blackballed, shouted at, given the 'I don't know how you can do this to me' treatment. Clare was a teacher in a small school who regarded me as a threat the moment I arrived. When it became clear that I would not be drawn into her 'gossip circle', then I was out, verbally bullied and subjected to malicious rumours.

I suspect that many entrepreneurs are Defenders. Their ego prepares them well for the ruthless cut-and-thrust of business. They are habitually distrustful of others and can sniff out the slightest whiff of danger in a deal. They are shrewd and cunning. On the other hand, they often find ways to create strong loyalty around them—but woe betide anyone who falls out of that circle of trust!

Behind the Defending strategy lies a sense of powerlessness. It involves not only little trust in others, but also little trust of self. Children who experience unreliable care will often conclude that the reason X doesn't remain on their side is because of a problem in themselves—it is *their* fault, they are to blame. Thus, they internalize the message that they, too, cannot be trusted. Sadly, Defenders find it hard to trust both others and themselves to be able to secure a long-term relationship.

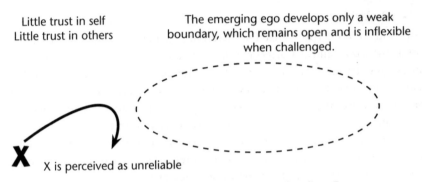

Little trust in self
Little trust in others

The emerging ego develops only a weak boundary, which remains open and is inflexible when challenged.

X is perceived as unreliable

Diagram 10.1   The pattern of the Defending Ego

The Defending Ego and leadership

For the Defender, life is about stopping people from hurting them. They long for secure, loyal, intimate relationships, but sometimes prevent themselves finding them by ending a relationship the moment there is any doubt or hint of rejection. They often frustrate their own longings and sometimes seem willing to sacrifice both themselves and others in a cycle of destruction and loss. How, then, does this ego work out in leadership?

Respect and suspicion

Defenders offer people one of two things: respect or suspicion. As leaders, they will tend to gather round themselves people to whom they are deeply loyal—perhaps being willing to accept a judgement or a piece of advice apparently on the basis of who gives it, rather than on its actual merits. They will tend to signal that they value loyalty, perhaps in both explicit and implicit ways. 'It's great to have you on board, Tom. You see, we're a close family here...' (Whoa! You thought you were joining a team, not a family!). 'Jane, we have very few rules in our department. What matters here is trust, simple, plain trust. We back each other up, see?' (It sounds great, but what's the subtext? If you show any dissent, or air an unpopular opinion, what may happen?) 'Mary, let me tell you how much I value you. You see, in the past we've suffered from people who've let us down. I know you're not going to be like them, so I want to let you into the plans we're making for where this ship is going...' (Great! You feel so privileged. But you also feel that I've somehow clipped your wings. It's much harder for you to show any dissent now that I've pulled you into this place of trust. And you didn't seem to have any choice in the matter, either. What happens if you don't want to be in here?)

Unpredictability

It should be no surprise that the Defending leader, who himself experienced unreliable care, tends to offer unreliable care to others. At times, you will be his greatest friend, a real insider, with all the benefits, and the warm feelings, that entails. And then, inexplicably, you will be pushed to the outside, for some perceived disloyalty, some minor betrayal, maybe insufficient enthusiasm for a pet project. Working for a Defending leader feels unsafe because you are on a knife-edge—and there's little you can do to change this, because being an insider is not, in a Defender's world, a matter of performance (which you can control) but a matter of threat (which you can't).

Corporate policemen

Corporations sometimes attract Defenders who act as corporate policemen to sniff out dissent—people for whom the organization is an extension of their identity. Disloyalty to the organization is disloyalty to them: it jeopardizes their whole world and they will not tolerate it. This, of course, can create a culture of mistrust. Their influence, though in the short term good for conformity and submission, is bad in the long term for humanity and health. For Defenders, the perennial issue of whether they can trust others rarely sets people free, because their freedom is contingent on their loyalty to their leader, not on truth or goodness. Of course, those on the outside may also be tarred inappropriately as enemies and so genuine, open collaboration becomes difficult. Partnership involves trust and real freedom, and for Defenders this is usually a challenge.

Leaders who are Defenders desperately need to be liberated from their sense of vulnerability. At their best, they can create strong communities that revolve around loyalty. At their worst, they can be suspicious and mean, willing to sabotage a project in order to protect themselves.

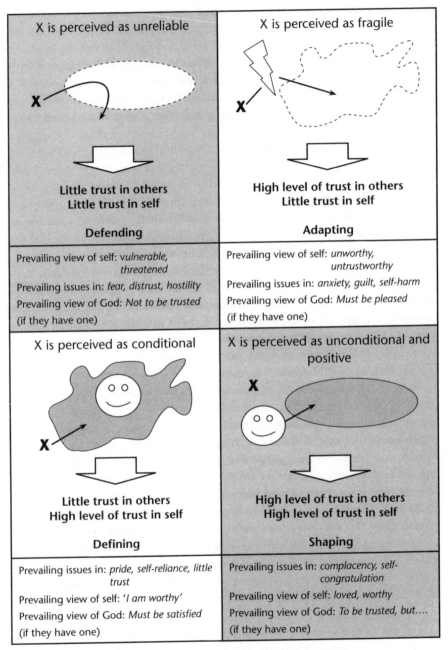

Diagram 10.2   Summary of Ego formation

Where does this in-depth discussion about the formation of egos leave us? We should recognize that no single pattern will define us. This is because the strategy we have developed on our back stage will be the obverse of the one we pursue on our front stage. If, for example, we show a high degree of trust in both ourselves and others on our back stage—the Shaping pattern—we will tend to show the opposite on our front stage: little trust in either ourselves or others, the Defending pattern. This seems a strange, contradictory conclusion to come to. How could this ever be true?

First, we must remember what this separation of two stages does for us. We develop a front and a back stage in order to manage our fear, to protect and promote ourselves in the world. Our performance on the stage is designed to secure a certain response from the audience. It should come as no surprise, therefore, that what we do on one stage is different from what we do on the other: our intention in developing these two stages is that this should be the case. It lies at the heart of our strategy, to reveal one thing but conceal another. The Adapter may choose to hide his vulnerable self away on his back stage and promote instead a self that is anything but: that is driven and focused and apparently confident—the Defining pattern. Or the Definer may choose to hide her need to avoid failure away on her back stage and show instead a more Adaptable, accommodating frontstage persona to divert the audience from seeing how much it all really matters. In fact, the four patterns work as two pairs: Adapting/Defining is one, and Shaping/Defending is the other.

Second, many of us know ourselves to be contradictory. Ask yourself this question: Am I entirely consistent? Your answer will be 'No,' because every one of us is inconsistent. We all say and do things that don't fit with our stated beliefs or our idea of ourselves. You may say you're a placid and laid-back person, and yet there are times when you lose your temper and fly off the handle. You may say you're a driven person, but there are situations in which you are lazy, self-indulgent and unfocused. You may say you're loyal in your friendships, but there are relationships you have allowed to break. None of us is consistent; none of us live up to our words. How refreshing, therefore, to find a reason for this! Contradiction—or, at least, paradox—lies at the heart of our strategy. We intentionally develop a side of ourselves, a persona perhaps, that is more concealed. It is real, nonetheless, a dimension of who we are, a theme in our story, an act in our drama. What a relief to find a way of making sense of its existence!

I often deal with leaders who suffer anxiety or guilt because a part of their lives doesn't match the rest. There are men with high sexual ethics who bewail the fact that they continue to give in to Internet pornography. There are confident women who crumble when they have to give a presentation to a meeting, their heart racing and their blood pressure rising. There are clergy who spend hours listening to the problems of church members and then come home and yell at their children and their spouse, who they love the most. There are executives who can confidently command boardrooms and oversee multi-million-dollar deals, but lack the authority and consistency to lead their families and win their respect. There are high-flying businesswomen who are bold and assured in all their professional relationships and comfortable in social gatherings and have flocks of friends and admirers, but who cannot, but cannot, let anyone into their inner fear and loneliness.

Contradiction is at the core of us, and to some extent will always be part of us. This shouldn't surprise us or worry us, and it is unhealthier to deny it than to acknowledge it. It has been observed of Churchill and Hitler that whereas the former was prone to excessive drinking, cigar-smoking and depression, the latter was a model of self-discipline and created a Reich that was intolerant of prostitution, gambling and all forms of unhealthy self-indulgence. And yet the unacknowledged contradiction within that one single life accounted for the murder of six million Jews. Beware the leader who has no knowledge of their own failings and who demands excessive purity! Behind the curtain may lurk devils too dark to show themselves. Devils tend to shrink when they are unmasked, and lose their power when they are named. I am not consistent, and you are not consistent, and it is better that we admit it.

So, where have we got to? We set out to find the root cause of our defendedness and we have located it right under our noses. It is our very selves that we are defending. At its most basic, we are not defending our jobs or our reputations or even our relationships: we are defending our egos. We are battling for our personal survival. Everything else represents the particular currency with which we have come to promote and protect ourselves in the world. As we have seen, there are four basic strategies of defence. In the Shaping strategy, the security of childhood ties remains intact and immunizes the individual from future feedback. In the Defining strategy, the continuing achievement of high standards defines the individual. In the Adapting strategy, the attraction of praise, approval and attention compensate for a lack of self-worth. In the Defending strategy, suspicion and loyalty are the keys to safety in a hostile world.

Underlying each strategy is an experience of trust—the degree to which we trust ourselves and the degree to which we trust other people. And the root of our strategy goes down to our experience of being trusted and of trusting others while we were growing up. The question is: Can we change? Can we ever be different from what and who we are now? Can we escape the patterns that have become embedded so deeply over the years and truly learn to live differently? Can we be liberated from the recurring attitudes and anxieties that have plagued us all our lives?

The answer to that question must be a resounding yes! I do believe we can be set free; I do believe we can be changed. If I didn't, I would have hesitated to write this book, for fear of raising expectations only to dash them. However, I do not believe that the answer lies within our own ability to change. Categorically, I believe it is not possible for an individual to will themself to change. I do not subscribe to the psychology that suggests that we have all the potential we need inside ourselves. The solution does not lie within. It can't lie within us, because the problem did not originate and does not lie within us. The root of our problem does not consist in some flaw in our character which we may be able to fix—no, it lies, and has always lain, in the formation of our relationships with others. What has been distorted, and continues to be so, is our experience of ourselves in relationship: the space we create between ourselves and others, the kinds of attachments we continue to form, the patterns of trust, or distrust, we establish. The problem lies not within us, but between us and others. And therefore the solution must also lie, not within us, but between us and others.

The solution must lie, in fact, in locating relationships with the world, with others and perhaps, uniquely, with Another, in which we are both trusted and able to trust. What we need are sources of love, affirmation and affection that can make us safe, can secure us against negative experiences in our own fragile histories: sources that are big enough, secure enough and unconditional enough to make us safe regardless of the threats that surround us.

Study questions 10

1. What childhood influences form a Defending Ego?
2. What characteristics does a Defending Ego display in terms of
   - behaviours?
   - attitudes to others?
   - attitudes to themself?
3. What leadership characteristics tend to be seen in a Defender?
4. How is the Defending Ego expressed on
   - the front stage?
   - the back stage?
5. Who have you experienced as a Defending leader? What was their impact on their followers
   - positively?
   - negatively?

PART III
THE SECRET OF THE
UNDEFENDED LEADER

ELEVEN

The Freedom to Fail: Locating the Source of Approval

Imagine you are performing Shakespeare for the first time on Broadway. This is your big night, something you seem to have prepared for and looked forward to all your life. Out there are waiting hundreds of expectant theatregoers, all knowledgeable and informed about what they like and don't like. Out there, too, is a hostile gang of theatre critics, ready to write their acerbic assessments of your performance, reviews that may determine the success or failure of your show, if not your career. Adrenalin is pulsing round your veins. The threat of potential failure and judgement makes your hair stand on end, your pupils dilate and your stomach twist into knots.

Now imagine that you hear a whisper from a stage hand: 'So-and-so'—a famous actor—'is backstage and wants to meet you!' You scarcely believe it, until you hear a knock at your dressing-room door and sure enough, there is the great man himself! He introduces himself and explains that he was in town and wanted to see you perform. He's heard such things about you and, from what he has seen on screen, senses that you have a great gift. He tells you that, whatever happens tonight, whatever tomorrow's papers say, he will be clapping you all the way.

Wouldn't the way you act this night be totally transformed by that one, single encounter, those few hurried words? The encouragement you had been given, the affirmation and unconditional support would change your experience from one of fear and anxiety to one of excitement, and perhaps even calm. What would be different, of course, is that the sense of threat had gone. The threat of the audience and the critics would be replaced by the safety of approval and an evaluation you respected more than any other. Indeed, even if your performance got the thumbs down from the critics, the sight of that one smiling, clapping figure in the stalls, the person who mattered most, would banish the fear of that criticism. It wouldn't necessarily improve your performance, but it would set you free.

Freedom comes from knowing that you are approved of. Freedom to perform comes from the knowledge that there is someone rooting for you in the audience, whose opinion you value more than anyone else's and who is smiling and cheering just for you. In such a relationship you become free from the need to succeed. Indeed, you can perform with nothing to lose, because you are secure that your identity, your future, your wellbeing, does not depend on the quality of your performance.

In the 2000 Olympics in Sydney, Jonathan Edwards had the weight of destiny resting on his shoulders. Some five years earlier he had broken the world record three times in his event, the triple jump, and since then he had been far and away the best triple jumper the world had ever seen. His record distance of 18.29 metres had never been challenged—no one had even come close. Season after season, he dominated the event. And yet, somehow, at the 1996 Games in Atlanta he had contrived to lose. 2000 was to be his year. He also acknowledged that this was going to be his last Olympics—his last opportunity to establish himself in his rightful place before he retired. Conventional sporting wisdom would have it that Edwards should have prepared mentally by eliminating the possibility of failure from his mind. He should have played over in his head, again and again, the image of himself jumping the perfect jump and winning the gold.

But that was not how he prepared. Instead, he contemplated defeat and stared it right between the eyes. Instead of blocking out failure, he chose to embrace it: he chose to embrace the idea of loss and reflect on what it would actually mean for him never to win the Olympic title. And when he considered that future, he discovered that it was not the threat he had feared it to be. He realized that he could survive such an outcome: he would still know who he was and, indeed, being a man of faith, his identity and worth in God's eyes would still be intact. In short, he found that his sense of who he was did not depend on how he performed as an athlete. In the event, Edwards ran down the runway free of fear, won convincingly and was rewarded with the medal he deserved.

Freedom to lead depends on us finding a source of unconditional approval that is not jeopardized by our performance. Leadership, like acting on Broadway or jumping in an Olympic final, is a threatening activity, one in which we may be observed and evaluated by a host of critics. As long as we fear the reaction of this audience, we can't be free in our leadership. Freedom comes when we are concerned only about the opinion of the one in the audience who truly matters.

As long as we fear for our job, as long as we fear for our salary, as long as we fear for our reputation, as long as we fear for our popularity, as long as we fear for our credibility, as long as we fear for our wealth, as long as we fear for our control, we cannot be truly free in our leadership. We will defend ourselves against the loss of the asset we value most. Only the person who is secure against the loss of all these things can be truly undefended, truly free. The secret of effective leadership is the freedom to live an undefended life.

Conventional wisdom insists that, in leadership, success come from dismissing the very idea of failure. The leader is the one who, through diligent training, preparation and foresight, can face any eventuality. The British Army supplies its officer cadets as they begin their training at the Royal Military Academy at Sandhurst with a little red book entitled *Serve to Lead*. Compiled in the 1950s, the book has a consistent message: that the leader is the one who is not threatened by failure because he has at his disposal tremendous resources. In short, he has mustered his defences, material, physical, mental and spiritual. The Army prizes defended leaders and trains men to become defended leaders. Arguably, this is the kind of mentality you need for combat. I often take former army officers through my course on undefended leadership, and I recall one describing the process as a kind of 'reprogramming'. Instead of controlling and suppressing his fear through competence, preparation and control, I was inviting him to trust that his ultimate security is assured, by a relationship that cannot be destroyed, even by bullets or bombs.

The idea of undefended leadership is that we are secured not by our skills and resources but by our attachment to another—one who is big enough not to be overwhelmed by our failures and weaknesses. Imagine that you walk into a room and find it full of all the people you have ever known. They are all there—all there because this is a party for you. As you enter, they turn and smile and welcome you, and you find yourself walking through a throng of friends. Music is playing and the air is full of chatter and laughter. Stories are being shared and connections made. There is apparently plenty of time to talk with everyone you want to and you converse with friends and relations, heroes and neighbours. Some you haven't seen for many years, and some you left on bad terms the last time you met; and there are conversations that need to be finished, or even begun. You realize that this room sums up your life, your presence in the world, for it contains all the people you have touched and affected in some way or another. Inside, you experience a wonderful, warm glow as you feel known and cared for and understood.

Slowly, one by one, the guests start to leave, and the room begins to empty. The music quietens down and you are left with your family. The host of memories and stories you share is like treasure—treasure that you gave them to cherish and look after: your deepest, most significant, most vulnerable being. The cracks where it has been dropped in the past remind you of the fragility and the pain you felt in earlier, unhappier times. But today, it seems, is not to be such a time. Today, you are held carefully and with respect, and you feel secure.

Finally, they, too, begin to go, one by one, and you are left, standing alone.

'Hello there,' says a voice. You turn and there, leaning against the wall, is a young man, smiling. 'You haven't seen me before, but I've seen you. Or, should I say, I've been watching you, since—oooh, well, since before you even existed, actually. I knew you when you were no bigger than a plum, growing inside your mother's womb. You see, I was there. I was there with you.

'I was there in the room when you were born, when you took your first gasp of air. I was there in those early months—I know what happened to you, I saw inside you, the things you couldn't see. I saw your fear when you were left alone and your joy when your mum returned. It was like an explosion of warmth inside you, swamping your little body. I was there when your first tooth came—and when the first tooth fell out. I saw you take your first step, and when you screamed with pain that day when you fell on your nose. I watched your hair grow. I watched it being washed and cut. I was there at the school gates when you went in, aching and scared inside where no one else could see. I knew your first house. I was there at your birthday when you were given that toy you had asked for and asked for.

'I was there, too, when you thought no one else was looking, no one could see. Yeah, I saw it all. I was there when you thought no one knew or cared or understood, in the night when you were alone, crying inside. I felt it with you. I have felt everything with you. And, now, I know what you do—each morning, when you wake, how you feel about the day, and about yourself. I know what it means for you to face another day. I have been there at your greatest victories and your greatest defeats. I have watched your life take shape. I've watched as you've hidden those parts of you away; I know the scars, and that surge of anxiety when that person comes near. I know what you long for in the deepest part of your being. I know what you believe you can achieve, and I know the frustration you feel at not being able to do it. Each night, I hold one by one your regrets for all the mistakes you have made, and I hold the shards of your shattered hopes so that they don't fall to the ground.'

He pauses and then says your name, and he says it as if he knows it very well—as if he has been saying it for years. 'I came here because you need to know one thing: that to me you are the most special and precious person in the world. And you need to know that whatever happens to you now, in the rest of your life, nothing will change that and you will never be alone.'

Freedom to lead an undefended life, freedom to lead others as an undefended leader, involves finding a relationship like that. A relationship in which we are safe, secured by an unconditional regard and affection, an unbroken attachment, that holds us despite the threats we face. As someone has said, it is another kind of defendedness, in which we are defended by Another rather than by our own strategies. It should be clear by now that even the best of relationships and attachments leave a legacy—a deficit. Even the most secure Shaper will be in danger of abusing others, and will one day face the fragility of losing her relationship with X. Human relationships are simply not big enough. They are not strong enough to survive death, or true enough to give us a proper sense of perspective, a proper sense of ourselves.

What I need is for an X to come and pour into me the love and acceptance I have craved. I need an X to say to me: 'I know what you're like and I still accept you.' I need an X who will always be in the audience rooting for me. I need an X who, even when I blow it, will come backstage, talk through the things that went wrong and tell me how to get up on my feet again. I need an X whose commitment to me is so tough, so strong that it can survive the worst I can do. I need an X in whose presence I feel utterly secure—when I'm with them, I don't need to worry about what others think of me or how I appear or whether I'm successful or not. I need an X whose view of me is true and fair and unbiased. I need an X who will lay out a pathway to the ideals and values that should direct me, but even when I fail to achieve them will not condemn me or cast me off. I need an X who is bigger than me, and bigger than all my worries—and that includes my boss, my relationships, my ambitions, my needs, my financial anxieties. I need an X who knows and understands my hopes and dreams; who will hold them and nurture them with me, and for me, and not drop them and let them break. I need an X who can work with the broken Simon as well as the whole and healthy and confident Simon.

Of course, the X I am talking about can't be human—at least, not merely human. This X has to be divine—but they also have to be personal. An X that is merely a force or a way of being or an organizing principle in the world is no good to me: I can't be loved and accepted and approved of by a cosmic energy. I need an X who is *for* me, not in a sloppy, sentimental, cuddly-grandfather way, but leading me on to greater things, better things, higher things. I need an X who is big enough to know and hold me in my suffering, but also hold the world in its suffering. An X who merely avoids looking at or dealing with injustice is no good to me, or to anyone. I need an X who takes evil and injustice, abuse and pain seriously, an X who sets boundaries, but safe, secure ones.

If I can find such a relationship, it will begin to make courageous, self-sacrificial leadership possible. Choices that previously were unavailable to me because they would jeopardize my success or reputation, will now become available because I won't need to safeguard my success or reputation.

Of course, the impact of such a relationship will vary according to which of the four ego patterns a leader manifests. Its impact on a leader with a Shaping Ego pattern will be different from that on a leader with an Adapting, Defining or Defending Ego pattern. The security and intimacy of such an attachment will penetrate to the very heart of our defendedness.

The Shaping Ego

Key transforming truth: The world is neither as safe nor as unsafe as you think.

Shapers believe that the world can be truly safe—on their terms. However, this is something of a fantasy, and the reality a Shaper needs to discover is that the world is neither as safe nor as unsafe as they feel it to be. The Shaper needs to grow up into a more mature understanding of life in which problems may remain unresolved and mysteries unsolved, and in which relationships may break down irrevocably. Instead of seeking a harmonious world, from which, under their governance, every disorder is eliminated, the Shaper must learn to tolerate difficulty, division and diversity.

Likewise, the Shaper may at times feel bitterly betrayed by people close to them who they trusted. The Shaper must learn to move beyond recrimination, to learn from the breakdown and to choose to trust others once more, but with greater discernment.

Key action: Stop trying to rescue people.

Shapers tend to act instinctively as rescuers, to try to save people from experiencing pain. In so doing, they prevent people taking responsibility themselves. They can also become burnt out in the process. Shapers need to restrain their impulse to fix, and instead must learn to be with others in the mess they're in and help them to shoulder their responsibility rather than trying to take it away. At the same time, they must allow others to give to *them*, to see their own need. As they do this, Shapers will become more sensitive to the complexity of the pain around them and will eschew simplistic, superficial or premature solutions in favour of the goals of maturity and wisdom.

Key attitude: Allow feedback to touch you.

Shapers find it all too easy to allow feedback to bounce off them. They may listen, but they often don't hear. As they are led into freedom, a Shaper begins to give a more open account of themselves, to tell a story of failure as well as success, problems as well as results. They choose to take responsibility for a sense of self that is not all sorted and secure but is being defined each day by their choices. Feedback from close colleagues and friends is an important source of material that they are eager to incorporate into their unfolding story.

The Shaper can make this journey into freedom only with the support of that secure relationship in which their need to defend themself is slowly dismantled.

The Defining Ego

Key transforming truth: You are not as successful as you think you are—but you cannot be as unsuccessful as you fear.

Definers live with a carefully nurtured sense of self, defined by exceeding personal standards and targets. Within that range, they can be extremely confident—in fact, over-confident. However, beneath that confidence lurks a fear of failure, and Definers need to be freed from this. They need to be released from the fear that their identity and worth will be devastated if they fall short of these standards. They need to be liberated from the sense that other people's affection for them is conditional on their good behaviour.

Instead of seeking to maintain their performance, Definers must discover the freedom to fail, to learn that they can fail and survive. They need to acknowledge their failures rather than burying them in denial as they are tempted to do. (Audit the things about yourself you're tempted to deny if you don't believe me!) They need to articulate their failures as part of the story they tell themselves and others. They need to live happily with both success and failure. As they do so, they will discover that they never were quite as good as they thought they were—but it doesn't matter as much as they thought it did anyway.

Key action: Stop wanting to win at all costs.

Definers find it hard to let others win. They are instinctively competitive, whether it be to do the shopping in the fastest time, to be the youngest person to reach that level in the firm or to be the only one to hit their targets that quarter. This can make it difficult for them to take pleasure in other people's success, or to seek win-win outcomes. Others around them may feel dominated and overwhelmed by their superiority, rather than empowered and enabled. Definers must consciously restrain their impulse to win while others lose, and should try out the experience of allowing others to win for a change. Most of all, they should look for win-win outcomes. Collaborative success through partnership should be the hallmark of their leadership: if they aim for this, they will not go far wrong.

Definers should also watch out for the activities they simply 'opt out of' because they secretly fear they can't win at them. Having a go at things at which they are less than the best is an excellent way to grow in freedom.

Key attitude: Enjoy the moment and stay in it.

Many Definers live entirely in the future: What is the outcome going to be? Where is the next challenge? How can I beat the competition in the next quarter? Once I've got this promotion, then I'll be able to invest time in my family… As a result, they often fail to appreciate the moment, the here and now. Definers who want to walk into freedom need consciously to resist the urge always to be moving on and living for tomorrow. Instead, they need to cultivate an awareness of what is happening now. This involves developing the ability to listen to their body, to notice how people are feeling in the office today, to enjoy their successes and celebrate them—as well as stay in touch with their feelings of fragility and inadequacy. As they do so, their experience of life will be much richer, and others will find their leadership more liberating.

The only route to freedom for the Definer is the daily appropriation of a source of affection and approval that is unconditional.

The Adapting Ego

Key transforming truth: Relationships are not as fragile as you believe.

Adapters live with the fear that relationships around them may fracture. As a result, they pursue strategies that are designed to shore up those relationships, which may involve attention-seeking, self-containment or acquiescence and accommodation. The long-term outcome can be exhaustion, anxiety, self-neglect or even self-harm. Adapters need to be set free from this fear of fragile attachments and the low self-esteem and self-trust that it produces. Instead of living to preserve something they fear may be taken away, they need to learn to trust themselves as people who are worth knowing.

As they grow in self-trust and self-respect, so they will be less afraid of what others may think of them. They will begin to believe that when they offer people their friendship they are actually offering them a valuable gift. They will begin to be able to say no to the demands of others and respect their own boundaries and limits.

Key action: Say no.

Adapters find it incredibly hard to say no. They fear rejection if they do so, they fear that the relationship will break if they don't always make themselves available. As a result, they are often exhausted themselves as they are used and abused by others: the firm, the family and the like. For Adapters, there is no more important choice than simply to choose to say no. This is a matter of respecting yourself and recognizing your limits. It is not self-indulgent, it isn't something you should feel guilty about. Often by saying no you help the other person to take appropriate responsibility: they benefit as a result, and (more important) so do you.

Adapters should recognize that their instinct is to take too much responsibility for problems around them, often blaming themselves for things that go wrong. Their route to freedom is to take less responsibility and ensure that others take more.

Key attitude: Trust yourself.

Behind this difficulty in saying no lies a lack of self-trust. Adapters often live with scripts that say such things as 'I don't merit their friendship,' 'If they really knew what I was like…' and 'I don't deserve this gift.' Their source of freedom lies in listening to the voice that says: 'You are of value because I love you.' These words are hard for them to hear and receive, but heard and received they must be. If you are an Adapter, write them beautifully on a sign to put on your desk, or make them your screensaver. And whenever someone offers you a compliment, don't just shrug it off and forget about it: treasure it as a genuine and precious gift! Write it down, put it in a beautiful box along with all the other gifts of approval and affirmation you have been given. It's time to start prizing the praise.

The Defending Ego

Key transforming truth: You are safer than you realize.

Defenders live in the expectation of an imminent breakdown in relationships. They are on the alert for it, anticipating it—and often actually making it happen by pushing other people into a corner. If you have been let down many times in the past by people you trusted, needed, relied on, it's easy to fear that the same thing is about to happen to you again—and that fear can drive Defenders to lash out before it's too late.

As they grow in confidence in the one relationship that will not let them down, Defenders will begin to be free from this fear. It is a question of where they turn their attention: towards the relationships that may let them down or towards the one in which they're secure.

Key action: Stay in the relationship.

The route to freedom is no quick fix, but instead is a settled, determined choice to restrain the impulse to cut and run when people appear to be disloyal or hostile. This takes courage—courage to confront your fear and not give in to it, to choose to take the risk of believing in others and yourself and offering your best. It involves accepting criticism without simmering with rage (or boiling over). It involves not withdrawing but continuing to offer yourself to be known.

Key attitude: Trust others.

As Defenders learn to trust themselves more, their highest priority should then be to trust others. Defenders fear that this is a great risk that leaves them exposed and vulnerable, but over time, as they discover that other relationships can be relied on, they will find that they are more able to take the risk of not withdrawing. If you are a Defender, make it a discipline to give trust away as much as you can. Choose to overlook the times when you have been let down and instead think the best of other people. As you discover what it is like to be trusted, in a trustworthy relationship, so all kinds of other trusting relationships will grow up around you. You will flourish and become welcoming, hospitable and generous, a 'safe place' not only for yourself but also for the many people who will be blessed through you.

Study questions 11

1. Which of the four Ego patterns do you most relate to?
   - Shaping
   - Defining
   - Adapting
   - Defending
2. In what ways does that pattern affect and determine your relationships
   - in your leadership?
   - with your family and loved ones?
   - with friends?
3. How much do you want to find a relationship that can secure you at the deepest level?

⊃ On the website, www.theleadershipcommunity.org, listen to the audio file with the 'visual landscaping' exercise 'Encountering God in your landscape'. This will help you to become more aware of being known by a spiritual source of approval. You need to be registered as a free 'guest member' in order to listen to the audio file.

TWELVE

The Freedom to Give: Cultivating Undefended Leadership

CULTIVATED
THROUGH...

9 ☒ 06

Robert K Greenleaf was born in Terre Haute, Indiana and spent most of his organizational life in the fields of management, research, development and education. Just before his retirement, he embarked on a whole new career and became a noted author. In 1970, he published 'The Servant as Leader', the first in a series of essays he wrote on the concept of the servant-leader.

Greenleaf argued: 'The servant-leader is servant first. ... It begins with the natural feeling that one wants to serve, to serve first. Then conscious choice brings one to aspire to lead. He or she is sharply different from the person who is leader first, perhaps because of the need to assuage an unusual power drive or to acquire material possessions. For such it will be a later choice to serve—after leadership is established.'[11]

---

[11] At http://www.greenleaf.org

As this quote indicates, the heart of the concept of servant leadership is that service precedes leadership. For anyone concerned about the moral condition of the world—and, indeed, the need for human beings to serve one another rather than exploit each other— Greenleaf's message is captivating. It cuts directly across the attitudes that prevail in so much of life and leadership in contemporary society. It insists on the moral priority of the other; it demands that leadership is not self-serving but other-person-centred.

The concept of servant leadership has been seized on eagerly by faith groups who find in it support for the vocation to service offered by the religious life. Many Christian authors have baptized Greenleaf's ideas, arguing that Jesus was the servant leader par excellence. Popular hymns have been written about Jesus the Servant King. A theology of leadership as service has readily emerged. This has, in part, been responsible for the strong emphasis in the last two decades that qualities of pastoral leadership are the most important attributes to look for in candidates for the ministry.

Greenleaf's message also resonates with the suspicions of postmodern and feminist critics that all acts of power are intrinsically oppressive: they disempower and restrict the liberty of others. In the light of this philosophical critique, leadership has been seen by many people as legitimate only in its posture as service—as something that is done from behind, from underneath, in the background. Essentially, leadership must meet the needs of others rather than dominating them and imposing the leader's own needs. As Greenleaf put it:

'As we near the end of the twentieth century, we are beginning to see that traditional autocratic and hierarchical modes of leadership are slowly yielding to a newer model—one that attempts to simultaneously enhance the personal growth of workers and improve the quality and caring of our many institutions through a combination of teamwork and community, personal involvement in decision making, and ethical and caring behaviour.'[12]

Greenleaf is not alone, nor even the first, to assert the primacy of service in leadership. As I have already mentioned, the British Army has been training its officers for more than half a century to 'serve to lead'. The notion of the leader who serves is quite deeply rooted in a military culture that prizes self-discipline, self-denial and the repression of emotion. There can be no doubt that the only legitimate goal of leadership is service. However, I wonder whether Greenleaf's very worthy and significant insights need to be developed a little further when we consider the context of social leadership.

---

[12] Robert K Greenleaf, taken from the introduction to Larry C Spears (ed), *Reflections on Leadership: How Robert K. Greenleaf's Theory of Servant-Leadership Influenced Today's Top Management Thinkers* (John Wiley & Sons, 1995)

I have had several years' experience of working with social leaders (including voluntary leaders)—some of whom, interestingly, have come out of the armed forces. In most cases, people give their time, skills and energy not in hope of reward or to advance their careers but out of a desire to do good. They exemplify, if you like, the kind of leaders for whom Greenleaf appeals. Furthermore, I have no doubt that many of them also applied the same mentality to their paid employment. However, in the course of working with a great number of such people and, indeed, being responsible for both their welfare and the welfare of those they led, I have encountered four problems.

The first is that some of these people are unable to give up their roles as volunteers when it is time for them to do so. What I have found is that, though they are willing and able, in service to others, to take these worthwhile roles, they find it much harder to let them go again. So often there are tensions when someone is asked to step down, when their leader suggests that a change is required. Then it becomes clear that, while they are ostensibly serving in this role for the benefit of others, they are also receiving something in return which they are unwilling to give up. If some such transaction was not taking place, they would be free to let go of the role when the community no longer needed them to do it. But they are not. The role makes up for some kind of psychological deficit they have within themselves. Perhaps it gives them an identity, perhaps it makes them feel valuable. Whatever it is, they are not free.

The second is that many people require affirmation or approval for everything they do. Of course, expressing appreciation is one of those things that all of us ought to do—there is rarely a person whose day is not brightened by a warm 'Thank you' or a grateful gesture. Cultures of positivity and praise are extremely important and I am not decrying them. However, it is important that we learn to lead others regardless of whether we are appreciated, regardless of whether we are thanked. When Winston Churchill lost the general election in 1945, many people, including his daughter, felt that it showed appalling ingratitude. Churchill himself took it hard. However, when he was asked once whether he resented it he replied that he did not, because he felt that the British people had suffered a lot during the war. Churchill experienced the sadness of being rejected but he did not blame those who did it and nor was he crushed by it. Many other people do and are, however. When they are not thanked for what they have given (freely), they are quick to complain. It seems that the appreciation they receive has become for them more than something they are simply free to enjoy. It has become a vital need, without which they can't thrive—without which they are reluctant to give more. In fact, it becomes clear that they are not serving freely but in order to receive thanks. Their service is not a gift but work to earn a wage of praise.

Third, there is the problem of those who cannot be served. Perhaps this is an aspect of those people I have already mentioned who can't give up their roles, but in this case they find it very difficult to receive from others. Many people in caring professions spend their lives giving to others but find it hard to be on the receiving end. It seems to be a place where they are uncomfortable. They are not, then, entirely free.

Finally, there are people who resent what they have given. Many volunteers and people in caring professions give for little return, but when someone feels bitter when they think of all they have given, something has gone wrong. Their service was not given as a gift but as a duty.

Many people in social leadership roles—for example, in health care, social work or community work—serve for reasons other than merely financial reward or preferment. It seems to me that Greenleaf's message is addressed to another kind of leader, the leader who habitually exploits others for his own personal gain. To this kind of person, Greenleaf offers a vital redress. However, in doing so I suggest that he opens the door to an alternative error: that the leader must somehow find within themself the love and grace to serve others. A significant percentage of people in social leadership, motivated by his vision of servant leadership, may fail to find these resources within themselves and instead run dry. So, they resort to constructing other kinds of collusion that secure them other, emotional rewards for their work. The danger in this is that not only will they end up exhausted and bitter but their followers will end up hurt.

I entirely approve of the high calling of leaders who serve rather than dominate and seek prestige. However, I am not convinced that Greenleaf is right to give serving priority over receiving. The British clinical psychologist Beau Stevenson describes a cycle of nurture and deprivation that can be found especially in those involved in the caring professions. He suggests that a high proportion of people in these professions have experienced homes where there is some kind of want. In such homes, a sense prevails that if anything is given away, it leaves a deficit. If, for example, a visitor came to the door unannounced, they would be duly invited in, but it would create anxiety about whether there was enough food to go round. The guest would be regarded as an inconvenience who would eat into the household's carefully rationed supplies. Their presence would 'take' from the family and leave a deficit. In contrast, in a culture of generosity the unexpected guest is welcome and the meal is gladly shared. It is not a duty or a cost. The guest is regarded as a blessing that brings something to the family that they are pleased to receive.

In the culture of deprivation, the transaction is one of taking and denying; in the culture of generosity, it is one of giving and receiving. In the first, the guest's presence leaves a gap; in the second, it represents a gift. Those who experience cultures of deprivation, Stephenson argues, grow up feeling a sense of obligation to make up for the deficit. The child feels the need always to give something to her parents in return for what they have given her. She grows up feeling guilty for the hard work they have to do, very grateful for every meal they provide, very overtly concerned when one of them is tired or ill. She learns that when something is given to her, she has to give something back. A transaction becomes established in which receiving always involves giving back. In time, as an adult, she comes to repeat this pattern. Serving others becomes the mechanism for earning appreciation. Stevenson suggests that such people are drawn to caring occupations in which they offer service to others. In return, they seek the appreciation of those they serve. I have encountered many people who conform to this pattern. In our terms, they fall within the category of either Definer or Adapter. They live with a sense that they and other people have to meet obligations. When these people enter leadership, it is usually social leadership and their motives are apparently philanthropic. However, in reality they do expect a return for their work—it's just not financial.

In contrast, those who grow up in a culture of generosity develop with a greater freedom. Their childhood experience is of resources abundant enough to supply their needs without leaving a deficit. There is enough love for them to be able to take it without feeling they have to pay for it in some way. Of course, there is no reason why someone used to plenty should want to give what they have away. They do not necessarily become generous just because they have experienced bounty. They, too, need to hear Greenleaf's message of service. However, it is clear to me that, as leaders, we can never give unless we have first received. Receiving should always come before giving. If that order is reversed, the gift becomes corrupted in some way. It tends to be given no longer freely but with strings attached.

Undoubtedly, the freest and most generous leaders I have come across are those from generous backgrounds. However, it does not need to be the nature of our home environment that determines our freedom and generosity as adult leaders: we must find and cultivate a generous source of approval elsewhere. As a Christian, I find that ultimately in God, who invites me as my divine Father back into a loving, intimate relationship. There are lots of striking observations in the Bible, but one of the most significant and extraordinary is the one Jesus is recorded as making in Mark's Gospel: 'The Son of Man did not come to be served, but to serve, and to give his life as a ransom for many.'[13]

The Son of Man—a reference to himself as God's anointed—comes as leader, not to be served but to serve. What the rest of the New Testament makes clear is that it is in the character of God himself to serve. Arguably the

[13] Mark 10.45

most unprecedented idea in the Bible, one with which I think we all have to wrestle, is this: that, unlike the Deity we are used to imagining, the God revealed in this book does not primarily demand to be served by us but instead seeks to serve. The God of the Bible is set on serving us, our needs, rather than on us serving him.

Now, of course, this God is no benign old man doling out heavenly favours to his spoilt children. Nor is it that humankind is so wonderful that in some strange reversal human beings themselves become divine. Rather, it is the compassion and unconditional generosity of God that compels him to reach out to those in need, even though they do not deserve it. This idea, of course, turns religion on its head. Religion is the social phenomenon in which human beings offer service to various divinities. According to Jesus and the writers of the New Testament, this activity of religion has nothing to do with God at all. God is not someone who is served, but someone who serves. If it is true that there is a personal God, who offers me love, affection, intimacy, acceptance, approval, simply because it is his nature and character to do so, then it is possible for me to receive from this source and so be free from needing others to give me these things.

This is like discovering a spring of fresh water that can begin to well up within you. Instead of having to make the effort every day to fetch water from various wells around about, a spring is available inside you which can pour out a stream of life-giving water. Indeed, this water can not only quench your thirst but can also flow out of you and be available to other people. Instead of leading out of our emptiness, there is the possibility that we can lead out of fullness. Instead of a deficit within us, that we make up through our success or power or influence, there is a fullness that meets all our needs, which we can offer to others as a gift. If this is the case, then it is possible that our leadership can change from being something that always in some way takes from others—as may happen to the servant leader—to being something that gives to others freely, in undefended generosity.

I love the story of undefended generosity told in the film *Babette's Feast*. In this tale, a female traveller arrives in a small, remote Lutheran community in Denmark. Her origins are mysterious and the closed community is naturally suspicious. It struggles to welcome this glamorous and flamboyant woman into its restrained and rigorous life. One day, Babette receives an unexpected letter, in which she finds a considerable sum of inherited money, and she decides that she is going to spend it on a great feast for all the villagers. She is, we learn, in fact a chef from Paris, trained in the finest cuisine. Over the next few weeks, strange parcels begin to arrive, containing all manner of exotic goods. The villagers are intrigued but also confirmed in their suspicions that Babette is a thoroughly dubious, worldly creature who does not know the discipline of spirit and body that their religion has taught them.

Finally, the day for the feast arrives and Babette invites all the villagers to come to her home. As they step in though the door, they are greeted by a world transformed. Instead of the grey ordinariness they have always known, there are colour and scent, and a stunning banquet of the most exquisite food laid out for them. There are even bottles of 'illicit' wine! Babette offers her hospitality to the villagers, who enjoy an evening they will never forget. She spends her entire inheritance on it, in a gesture of grace, generosity and freedom. Indeed, she spends herself, and in so doing she transforms her friends. During the meal, old rivalries and resentments, fostered for years between neighbours, are brought out and forgiven. Their eyes are opened and their own meanness and shrunkenness of heart, after years of self-denial, is transformed into generosity through the grace they receive.

My personal experience is that at the centre of the universe there is a God whose characteristic act is to give, to give freely, to give from limitless resources: who gives not in order to meet some need in himself but to establish relationship. So liberal is his creation that people who do not see a Creator behind it will still talk of 'the abundance of Nature', and may refer to the beauty, fertility and even love of the universe, which 'calls us into synchronicity' with the world around us. In such a world, we experience life 'coming to us as a gift'.

My two-year-old daughter likes to stand in front of me with a bag of crisps (or whatever she happens to be eating) and feed them to me, one after another. She puts her hand into the bag, takes out a crisp and offers it to me, watching expectantly as I take it, smile, say thankyou and eat it. Then she does the same again. Smiling, enquiring, enjoying giving to me. Doesn't she worry that the bag will run out and she'll have none for herself? Isn't she anxious about going hungry that night? Not at all! She hasn't given it a moment's thought! It never occurs to her that she may not be given all her stomach needs to be satisfied. Because she lives in a home blessed with plentiful supplies of food, she has never known what it is to be without; and so she trusts, and receives, and gives.

However, there is a choice to be made. Do we choose to experience life as a possession that may be taken away from us, or as a gift generously bestowed on us? For the leader who sees her life as a possession, leadership is a matter of acquiring more. It means protecting her assets and watching out for threats. It means maximizing her investments and exploiting opportunities. It means being tied to a plan, because you can't be still, listen to the moment and move where you need to. It means working with others only when self-interest dictates. It means a life ruled, ultimately, by a creeping, gnawing fear of what she might lose and a hunger for what she could gain. There is, of course, great motivation to be found from such a choice—fear motivates, as we have seen in the Defining and Adapting patterns, and it creates great drive. But the consequences may not be the freedom and peace that we seek, and that others we lead also seek.

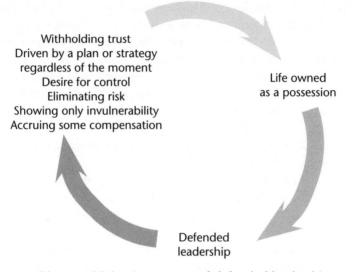

Withholding trust
Driven by a plan or strategy
regardless of the moment
Desire for control
Eliminating risk
Showing only invulnerability
Accruing some compensation

Life owned
as a possession

Defended
leadership

Diagram 12.1   A summary of defended leadership

In contrast, choosing to receive life as a gift leads to a very different set of consequences for the leader. Leadership becomes a matter of energetically joining in a movement of life and love around us that is already in full flow. A matter of finding ways to encourage and cultivate the gifts of others. A matter of choosing to trust others and take the risk of setting them free to succeed and fail. This leadership resists becoming merely executive management and instead remains attentive to the critical decisions of the moment, able to adapt and choose the right thing to do. It is not possessive about achievements. It is playful and compassionate and generous with praise.

When I ask groups of leaders to list the two things that would change if they started to act as an undefended leader, the things they suggest are very simple, even obvious. These are some of the things that come up time and again:

· Experience less duty and obligation around key tasks
· Celebrate more!
· Ask for help, work in teams and become dependent on others as often as possible
· Go to bed earlier
· Play more sport
· Get excited about stuff

- Be chaotic and messy
- Revel in each new discovery made
- Enjoy freedom of emotional expression
- Enjoy the moment
- Rest!
- Be intrigued by people
- Go for every exciting adventure you can
- Go into every day not knowing what to expect

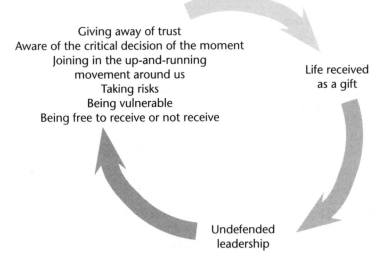

Giving away of trust
Aware of the critical decision of the moment
Joining in the up-and-running
movement around us
Taking risks
Being vulnerable
Being free to receive or not receive

Life received
as a gift

Undefended
leadership

Diagram 12.2   A summary of undefended leadership

We could extend that list endlessly, and you will already be adding your own suggestions. The funny thing about this list, whenever my groups compile it, is how liberated and excited it makes people feel just to think that some of these things could actually become a reality in their lives. It is almost as if they dare not believe it is true. But it is true! A veil has been cast over our eyes to make us believe that the world is one of duty, fear and self-protection. We must choose to tear away this veil and see a different world. We must choose to inhabit a world that is basically generous and make a commitment to trust ourselves to it. As we do so, the kind of leaders we are will change inevitably—change without any great effort or strain, without us learning new techniques or going on more training courses. The question is: How much do we want it?

We shouldn't confuse liberty with licence, however. In saying that change will happen to our leadership without effort or strain, I mean that, once we deliberately choose, and go on choosing, to live in the world 'as a gift', changes in our leadership will inevitably flow from that freedom. However, we should be under no illusion: attaining that way of being in the world requires intention, will and discipline. Discipline in leadership is often taken to involve a subjugation of your own instincts and feelings for the sake of a greater goal. There is something subtly different about the discipline an undefended leader requires: it is needed to prevent the defences reforming. Our defended way of being in the world is deeply embedded in us, like a habit or even an addiction. Ask a junkie what self-discipline is involved in coming off the substance they have depended on for years! They will tell you that the hardest thing is to say no to the continual, relentless urge to assuage your cravings by resorting to the drug again.

The greatest thing our defendedness gave us was a sense of security and control, and so the moments when we feel insecure and out of control will be when we are most tempted to resort to those strategies once again. Those are the times when we will reach for a shot of attention to give us that boost when our confidence is low. Those are the times when, with a shaking hand, we will pour ourselves a tumbler of success laced with the CEO's praise and a pay rise. Those are the times when we will inhale deeply the smoke of corporate denial and chicanery to enjoy the high of complicity and the rush of power.

Living as an undefended leader is a matter of cultivating an undefended life, deliberately and with discipline and focus, over years, not months. The specific choices we need to make will always relate to the particular pattern of defendedness we have embedded in our egos.

In order to sustain an undefended life, *Shapers* need to choose

- to set extra time aside when appraising their staff so that they can genuinely listen to them and create space for their personal and emotional stuff to be heard rather than being suppressed for the sake of the corporate goal;
- to be honest about an issue they are struggling with in the boardroom, risking vulnerability but inviting empathy and creating an opportunity for a humanizing encounter to take place;
- to be committed to a relationship that has lost its sparkle, because they have made vows and promises to do so.

Definers need to choose

- to make changes to their frenetic routine, planning in times to retreat and receive a renewal of their sense of identity and approval;
- to let go of a possession that has become an idol that enslaves them: a car they love, a treasured role, a carefully nurtured ambition...;

· not to read the business press so obsessively, or to get the latest downloads of the market on their mobiles every hour, but instead to trust that if they spend the time they gain reflecting and waiting, it will prove a better guide to their decisions;

· to let go of some habit they have relied on, something that is not bad in itself but has become a crutch, perhaps an exercise routine they observe religiously, or a diet.

Adapters need to choose

· to switch off their mobiles and be unavailable at times they have set aside to play, or pray, or be with their family;

· to resist the urge to plough into their e-mails at the start of the day without first stilling themselves and handing over all their fears and hopes to their source of safety;

· to hand over to someone else a role they have become possessive about: perhaps a department, or a ministry in a faith community, or the chair of a council;

· to ask for help when they need it, rather than taking on all the responsibility themselves.

Defenders need to choose

· to put themselves in unfamiliar and even frightening situations at work that they would naturally avoid, in order to experience the freedom of being undefended by their normal skills and scripts;

· to notice their emotions as they arise, taking responsibility for their fear or anger rather than allowing them to dominate them and dictate their reactions;

· not to try to manipulate their situation in order to preserve their status or reputation;

· to risk confrontation by being honest about their feelings without blowing up in an aggressive, out-of-control way.

Living out an undefended life as a leader by and large involves living in a place that feels provisional and perhaps uncomfortable. Beware the times when we feel competent in everything we do! I find myself impressed with the philanthropy of Bill Gates and Warren Buffett not so much because of the vast scale of the wealth they have both given away ($28 billion and $37 billion respectively) but because of what it represents: a willingness to embrace their humanity again— with a measure of vulnerability along with it. Beware our sense of mastery of our universe. Be sure that, if we ever experience this, or make it our goal, we are selling our souls to a false god. We will find ourselves serving only a reflection in a mirror, an idol with clay feet, who cannot make us truly safe or fulfilled. We will have been seduced by the illusion that life can be free of pain and difficulty, only to discover that we cannot, in the end, preserve ourselves from these.

Finally, I need to make it clear that I am not talking here about living a balanced life. You might read this chapter superficially and conclude that I am appealing for leaders to balance their lives. The call to avoid extremes of activity or passivity is a worthwhile one, but not one I am making here. On the contrary, I am calling for leaders to live extreme lives: lives that exhibit radical and risky characteristics shared by only a few. The choices you make to start to live an undefended life, to lead as an undefended leader, are made not for the sake of balance or wellbeing; they are made for a greater good. And that greater good is to set people free. The undefended leader doesn't live by a manual for wellbeing, nor does she aspire to a healthy balance as an end in itself; she aspires only to bring freedom wherever there is enslavement. At times, this results in the freedom to choose not to work, to choose not to be driven, to choose not to burn out. At other times, it issues in the freedom to exhaust yourself for the cause, to take huge risks, to set everything up to succeed or fail. What governs these choices is not self-preservation, or some notion of a stress-free and integrated life. Rather, it is born out of the conviction that only the radically undefended life is a free life; that only choices made to embrace the generosity of the world around us issue in abundant life.

This perspective also gives us a new angle on the often asked question: What is the difference between the task of leadership and that of management? Frequently, the answer is given that the leader is the one with vision and the manager is the one with hands to implement it. Sometimes it is said that the manager is the person who climbs up the ladder, efficiently and within budget, while the leader is the one who notices that 'the ladder is leaning against the wrong wall.' Other images are common. The leader has a 'helicopter perspective' and can see the overview. Or he is the one who climbs to the top of the mountain and from there he can see the workers working on every side, whereas they can see only the slope on which they themselves are toiling away.

Such metaphors are helpful enough, and encourage leaders to look for the bigger picture rather than a mere detail. What I think they are all reaching for is the sense that leadership is, at its purest, concerned with truth. In its highest calling, it is not concerned with pragmatic solutions, with getting the job done: it is a matter of seeing something more truly than others around you.

Many things darken and cloud the eyes of those who seek this kind of 'sight'. In the first place, as I have said, our own unmet needs distort our vision, determining the way we see things. Our own self-interest (as opposed to the interests and needs of others) muddies the waters we swim in. In the murk, people start to panic and thrash around, flailing after passing shadows, only stirring up more mud in the process. Stillness is what is needed if the mud is to settle and the waters to begin to clear. And this is the posture of the leader. While others are still urgently straining away, towards some unclear goal, the leader is the one who stops—and perhaps makes other people stop around her. And when she has stopped, she waits. And as she waits, she listens, and feels, and looks. And as she does so, shapes begin to emerge and the scene begins to become a little clearer.

Leadership has little to do with making lots of decisions, with getting a great deal done. It is about getting the right things done. As leaders, the crucial quality we need is the courage to stop. The courage to wait and be still. While everyone around us is clamouring for a decision, the leader waits until she is confident and clear.

Study questions 12

1. Why does this chapter suggest that the concept of the servant-leader may be problematic?
2. What kind of culture did you experience growing up?
   · a culture of deprivation?
   · a culture of generosity?
3. What kind of culture do you tend to create around you?
4. How would your life be changed for the better if you experienced the world as essentially generous?
5. What three changes would you make to your life to begin to live out an undefended life?
   a)
   b)
   c)

⮕ On the website, www.theleadershipcommunity.org, listen to the audio file with the 'visual landscaping' exercise 'Responding to needs around you'. This will help you to become more aware of how to experience the world as a generous place and how to receive from a source of generous approval. You need to be registered as a free 'guest member' in order to listen to the audio file.

THIRTEEN

Leading as a Child

The bullying had got worse and something had to be done. The problem was that the bully had the power and influence to make life hell for anyone who crossed him, and most people just accepted it and tried to avoid becoming a target. But one victim decided that, after all the racial and sexual abuse, the derision and humiliation, he wouldn't stand for it. He could have gone up the chain and lodged a formal complaint. He could have set disciplinary procedures in motion. He could have got revenge in more subversive and spiteful ways. But instead he chose another course of action.

He gathered the team together and found out how many others had had the same experience as him. Stories began to come out that had been kept quiet out of shame and fear of further victimization. As the full scale of the problem emerged, the collective anger grew, and a resolve that this had to be stopped. Everyone looked for a lead from the person who had called the meeting. 'We're going to confront this guy together,' he said, 'and show him this has got to stop.' So, they set a time and everyone agreed to be ready to tell their story.

The bully was invited to a meeting about something important that he should know about. When he walked in, he was shocked to find that it was about him. The door was shut and he was made to listen as person and person told the group what he had done to them. Then the appointed leader stood up. He told the bully that he had a choice. He could carry on as before, in which case he would find that everyone, every day, was against him. His requests would be ignored, his projects allowed to fail; he would eat alone and he would be excluded from every future assignment the group took on. Or he could apologize to each and every person he had hurt and write a statement saying how he planned to change. In that case, the group would agree not only to accept it but to help him to live up to it. The man's face crumpled as he recognized both the shame of his actions and the grace of the chance that was being given to him to come back into the group—but on new terms. He knew which option he wanted to take.

This story of leadership illustrates the power of the community collectively to deal with its own problems. Without resorting to expensive legal proceedings and the structures of bureaucracy, the problem was addressed and sorted out locally and directly. Instead of acting out of fear, the group chose to trust one another and, indeed, to trust the bully. Instead of seeking to defend themselves or to retaliate, they chose courageously to make themselves vulnerable. Different forces were brought into play, forces of social belonging, shame and guilt, forgiveness and acceptance, help and mutual support. These forces proved powerful enough to resolve the situation more quickly and less expensively than any formal proceedings could have done, and without the organizational damage.

Think how many millions of dollars in lawsuits would be saved if disputes in the workplace were solved like this. Think how many conflicts between warring communities would be resolved in weeks if a similar process was followed. Think what potential there would be to reduce violence and fear in the neighbourhood if communities would take that kind of collective responsibility. All it took was the mobilization of the forces of social belonging, shame and guilt, forgiveness and acceptance, help and mutual support. And a leader who was willing not to give in to feelings of hate, not to seek revenge, but instead to act courageously and make himself undefended. It took a leader who decided that trust was more powerful than fear. And he was right.

However, the thing that is most striking about this story is that the person who took the lead was not a business manager, a corporate executive or a community leader: he was an eight-year-old child. The whole thing took place in a classroom at a primary school.

I expect that that comes as a surprise. To some, it may even come as a shock. You might find yourself resisting its implications. 'Well, of course', you may say, 'the child didn't have much idea about what was really going on—it just happened to work out for him.' But isn't that just the point? A child is unaware of all the theory about why things do or don't work. He comes at things without years of experience and baggage, and sometimes that is just what enables you to see the situation as it really is rather than as you might have expected it to be. Our problem is our difficulty in seeing the world as it is and not through the distorting lenses and filters of our experience, knowledge and prejudice.

Or you may say: 'Well, it's easy for a child of eight—he hasn't yet had to cope with the knocks of life. He won't be so trusting of others after he's been let down a few times.' Once again, isn't that exactly the point? As adult leaders, we bring into every situation the baggage of our past. Indeed, we have spent much of this book exploring the architecture of that past and the legacy of (dis)trust it has left us. Of course, we can't undo the past, but we can become aware of it, and this allows us to reverse the strategies we have used to cope with that which enslaved us. It isn't difficult to appreciate the freedom the child had to face this situation. The question is not whether this is desirable—of course it is! The question is whether it is attainable for us, hard-bitten, cynical and defended grown-ups.

Or you may say: 'It was an unthreatening scenario—nothing like as nasty as things get in adult life! As leaders, we have to deal with people who threaten our very jobs, our salaries, our careers. We have to handle multimillion-dollar deals that will affect the lives of hundreds of employees. It's all very well being undefended when the stakes are so low; it's quite another matter when the stakes are so high!' And yet to argue like this is to miss the point. For a child, that bully was the embodiment of threat and fear. A child isn't aware of or concerned about global warming or the state of the market. They are concerned about whether they get assaulted in the loos or on the way home from school. What more direct threat do you want than that? In fact, the reality is that we, as adult leaders in the West, very rarely face a situation that is physically menacing. The threat of material harm, such as losing a job, is probably the biggest danger most of us would face in a decision we had to take. And you can recover from losing a job—we are fortunate enough to live in a society in which we would receive benefits. We probably have some assets, some savings. We probably have sufficient skills to get ourselves another job. In reality, the threat is not fundamentally threatening. Yet we make it so because we habitually avoid pain. In fact, the West has become a society bent on eliminating pain and struggle from our lives. When we are threatened in the slightest degree—by a loss of earnings, by not being able to go on holiday, by missing out on a promotion— we become anxious and depressed, fearful and defended. The point is that children are usually far less guarded about their own safety than grown-ups. Think of your average teenager bombing down a ski slope, past the cautious and rather genteel descent of the 'sensible' adults!

Or you may say: 'A child's an idealist. You can't be idealistic in life as a leader. Speak to any politician! Leadership is about pragmatism. There are no neat, black-and-white solutions—life is too complex and interconnected. Choices always involve shades of grey, compromise, give-and-take. Leadership in the real world is about being able to make those compromises and still come up with some kind of way forward.' Sure, the life we live is complicated and compromised—because we make it so. What guided that child was some basic values and principles of action which cut through the complications. It would have been far more complicated to file a complaint with the school authorities.

By acting locally and directly, the child actually simplified the task of leadership. Imagine if he had gone up the chain. What would have happened? First of all, a lengthy process of gathering data would have taken place. Teachers would have asked questions and conducted interviews, filled out forms and written reports. Meetings would have been called with the appropriate agencies. The bully's background would have had to be taken into account. Maybe social services would have been brought in. Maybe they would have concluded that the source of the problem was a dysfunctional home, a violent father who beat his mother, neglect and lack of love. Yes, the bully would have been more understood by adults if this process had taken place; but the solution would have been no better. Probably a behaviour therapist would have been sent in to 'work with the child' and support the teacher, an intervention that would have been costly and lengthy. In any case, it would only have been successful if the other children had been included in the process so that the procedures could be supported within the classroom—otherwise, the bully would only have ended up feeling more excluded and ostracized. In truth, the 'adult leadership' solution would have been more complicated, more time-consuming and more expensive—and would still in the end have had to rely on the same social and emotional mechanisms to solve the problem.

All this prompts the question: Is there any way in which a child offers us a model of what undefended leadership might look like?

Maintaining a light and playful touch

First and most important, a child does not think of themself fundamentally as a leader. A child thinks of themself as a child—a child who, in this situation, is doing a particular activity. A child's principal frame of reference is not learning, or leadership, or performance: it is play. Children engage with the world essentially through play. I can vividly remember making it to the national finals of the school hockey championships. My team had beaten all comers that season and we were going to play in a major stadium. Our nerves were jangling as we sat in the changing room before the match—the biggest sporting occasion of our lives to date, and possibly ever. Our coach looked at us and said: 'Now, there's one thing I want you to promise me to do when you get out there on the pitch today: enjoy it! Enjoy the next 80 minutes! This is a one-off experience, and the most important thing is not to miss it.'

Winston Churchill spent five years summoning the energy and self-belief to lead the British nation from 1940 to 1945 in resistance to the mighty forces of Germany and later Japan. Renowned for his inexhaustible energy and focus, Churchill almost burned out other, far younger ministers and aides, despite being in his late sixties. Not only was he battling Hitler but on the home front he had to contend with his deputy prime minister, Clement Attlee, the leader of the Labour Party. After a particularly grey and difficult few days, late one evening, when the news from Europe was especially disheartening and Attlee was being a thorn in his side, the lowering Churchill was seen to turn to his wife, Clemmie, and growl, 'Enough of Hittlee and Atler—let's go and watch a film, shall we?' Amidst the pressure of the greatest military conflict in history, he didn't lose touch with his childlike side. Known as a man who took his own destiny very seriously, he still managed to retain a sense of humour in the darkest hour.

Think about your challenges at work right now. Now think about how many of them have come to daunt or oppress or even overwhelm you. Now think about how some of them have taken on a sense of absolute reality—they have started to define your horizons. Now think about how that would change if you were to reposition those same challenges as if you were a child joining in with work that was actually his dad's responsibility. When a father invites his child to come and help him in the garden, he gives her a trowel and the child makes some scrapes and perhaps digs a few small holes for some seedlings. However, the reality is that the father doesn't need the child to get the gardening done— in fact, the job probably takes far longer with her 'help' than if he'd done it on his own! He invites her to join him not because he can't do it without her but because he doesn't want to. He delights to share this activity with his child out of the joy of 'working together with' her—for the sake of their relationship, their love, their fun, her learning.

Humankind has achieved astonishing things in its history, and we have seen astonishing men and women accomplish great tasks of leadership. But none of them are absolute; none of them surpass the great mysteries and deep beauties of the universe. Remember that your greatest achievement as a leader will not solve the world's problems. It will not bring about heaven on earth or save the planet. Make your contribution with a smile, thankful for the opportunity and delighted to see other people make theirs.

Retaining the capacity to wonder

It is said that in the course of a long evening of government business, Abraham Lincoln would lead his colleagues outside and there in the night sky he would point out a small smudge of light. 'That, gentlemen,' he would say, 'is the nebula Andromeda. It is the nearest galaxy in the universe to our own Milky Way. It is three million light years away. It is composed of more than a hundred billion stars, most of which are bigger than our own sun. It is one of more than a thousand million galaxies in the universe. Now that I think we feel small enough, we can go back inside.'

Wonder begins with awareness and could be said to be the basis of all leadership. Awareness is our ability to perceive ourselves and others and the world as we are. Self-awareness is the first of the competencies that constitute emotional intelligence. Awareness of the Other is the foundation of what some people have called 'spiritual intelligence'. But the valuing of awareness is much older than these new ideas. In the fourth century, the Desert Fathers, the pioneers of Christian monasticism, understood that awareness of the distorted nature of the self lies at the beginning of the journey out of that self towards *theoria* (contemplation). Ignatius Loyola's 'Spiritual Exercises', written in 1548, are based on developing an awareness of yourself within the accounts of biblical events. John Calvin, the 16th-century Swiss Reformer, asserts in his *Institutes of the Christian Religion* that Man never attains a true self-knowledge until he has previously contemplated the face of God. The purpose of meditation in Buddhism is to achieve a greater awareness of your desires and drives. Through awareness of your attachments, you are able to detach and so be 'free' from the illusion of this material reality. In Islam, the rhythm of daily prayer returns the individual to a God-consciousness amidst the activities of the day.

Children often exhibit a remarkable, naive awareness of themselves and their world. They tell you when their body hurts or feels hot or cold, they're conscious of fear, excitement, shock and loss in a more immediate way than we grown-ups. The journey into adult life often involves suppressing and dismissing feelings, which in turn lowers our body-awareness. Awareness of self is in dialogue with awareness of others and our world. As we become more aware of our participation in the ecology of life around us, we become aware of our appropriate scale, humanity and interdependence. Our mistake as leaders is often to think we are bigger than we really are. We come to believe, because we inhabit the small worlds of offices and institutions, that we are masters of our worlds. Of course, we are not—when a natural disaster strikes, we soon realize how weak and powerless we really are.

How our use of time, our priorities and our decisions as leaders would change if we retained a sense of wonder from moment to moment—about breath and molecules and photosynthesis and scents and birth and death. During the American Civil Rights movement in the mid 1960s, the aggressive Black Power movement arose in response to the apparent impotence of the black population and the violence and intimidation it was suffering. On 16 June 1967, Martin Luther King distanced himself from Stokely Carmichael, his friend and a former colleague in the Southern Christian Leadership Conference (SCLC). He refused to accept that, as Malcolm X proposed and Carmichael increasingly was advocating, the way to resolve political, economic and social injustice was through violence. At the heart of King's philosophy was his belief in the shared humanity and equal worth of black and white and his conviction that the solution was to find a way of mutual respect. Without a sense of the dignity of creation, King's ideology would have been susceptible to become a clarion call for domination. Wonder, rooted in an awed awareness of the world in which our lives are a gift we have received, does not lead only to poetic idealism: it also produces hard-headed politics, social strategy and some of the most courageous leadership of the 20th century.

Not that a leadership of wonder always issues in success! In 1982, Joe Montana, the stellar quarterback for the San Francisco 49ers since being drafted in 1979, went out on the pitch in his first Super Bowl. Inexplicably, in the midst of one 49ers drive, he stopped and just stood still. When the time limit for the play expired, he was fined a 10-yard penalty. After the game he was asked why he didn't get the play off—something a schoolboy quarterback would know to do—Montana replied that he decided he was not going to miss this great event, and in the midst of the game he was going to stop for a moment and just take it all in. Sometimes, life is just too wonderful to miss!

Strengthening the bonds of trust

Children trust. Implicitly. It's what makes them so vulnerable. I put my children in the car and we head off on a journey, and they simply trust that they will be safe, that there will be a meal provided, that they will have a bed to sleep in at the end of the day and probably some sweets along the way. As we grow, we learn to trust less. There are good reasons for this, but if we lose the ability to trust we lose the basis of all human relating. Robert Galford and Anne Seibold Drapeau's book *The Trusted Leader*[14] argues the case for the role of trust in organizations. They illustrate their point with numerous examples of companies whose performance falls when there is a systemic lack of trust in the firm. Trust involves risk—there is no legal safeguard. Trust involves making yourself vulnerable, putting yourself in someone else's hands; trust involves letting down the barrier of self-protection and allowing someone else to help us. Trust involves securing the relational bond between two people not by contract but by mere promise. Of course, in a culture where 'promise' means so little, trust is hard to come by.

Trust does things, though. Remember what it feels like to be trusted: trusted with a task, a treasure, a secret, trusted to keep a promise. When you are trusted by someone else you feel important: valued, respected, needed. Children who are habitually trusted by their parents develop a healthy trust of themselves and others, a positive self-regard. Children who are not trusted feel vulnerable and lack self-respect and self-belief. Remember what it feels like to be trusted. It feels good, doesn't it? As leaders, we can give that experience to another person this very week, this very day, this very hour.

Not only does trust make people grow, it also heals social ills and reduces the burdens on any civil society. In 1947, following independence, the subcontinent of India faced a massive and violent internal struggle. The majority Hindu and minority Muslim populations proved unwilling to coexist and, despite Gandhi's pleas that the land should not be divided, it was indeed partitioned and the states of India and Pakistan were formed on 14 August 1947. However, no one had envisaged the chaos that was to follow as literally millions of Hindus and Sikhs living in Pakistan began a mass migration across the new border into India, passing en route the millions of Muslims migrating the other way. Conflict erupted, and the ensuing bloodbath was catastrophic. In charge of the partition and the transition to statehood was Lord Mountbatten, the British Governor General of India, who positioned his troops at various flashpoints, and Delhi and Calcutta in particular. However, there was another force at work restraining

---

[14] Galford, Robert and Drapeau, Anne Seibold, *The Trusted Leader* (The Free Press: Simon and Schuster, 2002)

the violence: Mahatma Gandhi. Central to his campaign was the rebuilding of trust between the divided communities. In the heart of the fighting, Gandhi would walk, barefoot, from one village to the next. When he arrived at a village, he would find the Hindu and Muslim leaders and would invite them to live together under the same roof, guaranteeing the peace between their respective communities. If one Hindu was killed, he charged the Muslim leader to fast until the murderer was brought to justice; and vice versa. Gandhi's weapon was not the gun but the embrace. He compelled people to trust one another again and resist the suspicion that leads to fear, that leads to prejudice, that leads to hostility, that leads to bloodshed.

Mountbatten's forces were literally overrun by the scale of the violence. He dubbed Gandhi his 'one-man boundary force' and heard to remark: 'On the western front I have 100,000 crack troops and unstoppable bloodshed. On my east, I have one old man and no bloodshed.' Gandhi's one-man peace corps was to prove more powerful than the might of the Army in restraining violence, in town after town, by building trust and strengthening the bonds of humanity.

Learning to take responsibility

It's a basic lesson of the kindergarten that we ought to take responsibility for the consequences of our actions. Robert Fulghum begins his delightful little bestseller *All I Really Need to Know I Learned in Kindergarten* with a credo. He writes, 'These are the things I learned [at kindergarten]:

> *'...Clean up your own mess.*
> *'Say you're sorry when you hurt somebody.*
> *'Put things back where you found them...'*

Then he extrapolates: 'Think what a better world it would be if ... all governments had as a basic policy to always put things back where they found them and to clean up their own mess.'[15]

It's so simple, isn't it? It makes sense in the playground, but out in the big, wide world what seemed black-and-white dissolves into murky shades of grey. To lead in a childlike way may, to some, imply a lack of responsibility, or duty or obligation. Far from it! Children tend to have a straightforward morality and instinctive senses of right and wrong, duty and loyalty. It is as we grow up that these may get confused. Many leaders devise complex schemes to avoid taking responsibility—to avoid paying corporation tax, avoid the expense of disposing

---

[15] Fulghum, Robert, *All I Really Needed to Know I Learned in Kindergarten* (Ballentine, New York, this ed. 2003)

of the company's waste, turn a blind eye to the impact of their supply-chain control on their suppliers, ignore the effects of their products on the consumers who buy them, ignore the impact of their energy consumption on the planet.

The thing about taking responsibility as a leader is that it often breeds responsibility in those around you. Eleanor was not an obvious leader. As owner of the local newsagent, her life had been a simple one. She had never stood for the local council or played any kind of civic role. All she did was run her shop. One day, however, she decided she was going to take responsibility, for something very small but very important nonetheless: the litter outside her shop. She lived in a little town in north-west England called Middlewich, a town that was neglected by the local authorities and had consequently lost its self-respect. Walking down the small, narrow high street on a Sunday morning was like wading through a garbage tip—filthy and foul and stinking with the refuse of the night before. And it was not much better by Monday!

Eleanor began by taping a black binbag to the wall (the council provided no bins) with a misspelt handwritten sign requesting that shoppers throw their litter in the bag rather than drop it. Then she went next door and gave the neighbouring shop a bag and asked them to put it out. Next, she wrote to the council and asked whether Middlewich could have some proper, smart, new bins. Next, she began to talk to her customers about the litter problem, and pretty soon she had a band of locals equally fed-up and eager to make a difference. On Saturday mornings, you would see her Middlewich Clean Team out in brightly coloured rainbow tops clearing up the rubbish in the parks. Next, she got the council to put up hanging baskets in the summer and dared to enter the town in the Best-Kept Town in Cheshire competition. To everyone's surprise, Middlewich won—and not just the county title but the accolade of the North-West 'most improved town'. The miraculous change held good, and within two years Eleanor was meeting the Deputy Prime Minister and being asked to act as a consultant to other towns struggling to deal with poor social behaviour.

Eleanor did nothing more than decide to take responsibility. Others began to follow her lead and soon the entire culture had begun to change. It's all too easy to turn a blind eye as a leader and simply not see what is not convenient. Many of the big issues are not screaming out at you, slashing your market share: they are simply going on in the background. We pass them by and hope that someone else will take responsibility for them. There are probably places on your territory right now where that is happening. It's what happened at Enron. And WorldCom. And Abu Ghraib.

Not all children are the same...

	Shapers	Definers	Adapters	Defenders
Rather like....	*an eight-year-old who is 'comfortable in their own skin'*	*an intense and dutiful 21-year-old heir*	*an over-anxious 11-year-old who is eager to please*	*a wary 16-year-old*
Maintaining a light and playful touch	Often have no problem with this as they are generally not overwrought by their jobs.	Are often terribly earnest, intense and driven in their role. May lose sight of play altogether.	May feel guilty about play, assuming that all worthwhile work is in some sense costly and hard.	May be sceptical of such 'innocent' motives and unwilling to let themselves go.
Retaining the capacity for wonder	Are drawn to the unusual and the novel without necessarily dwelling too deeply on it.	Think that wonder doesn't get the job done, and probably put it off as a 'luxury' for a later date.	Probably suppress their sense of wonder in case it is disparaged.	May be very sensitive to awe as it feels 'big' and 'authentic'.
Strengthening the bonds of trust	Have no problem trusting others. In fact, they are probably too trusting and need to be more discerning.	Never give unqualified trust but believe that trust is earned through performance and success.	Find it very hard to ask anyone else to take things on, and as a result may prevent others from learning to trust themselves.	Are desperate to do so, but may demand such loyalty from other people that they can only disappoint.
Learning to take responsibility	Shoulder considerable weights, but may abdicate responsibility for harder and more uncomfortable tasks.	Want exclusive responsibility most of the time, but occasionally refuse to accept any responsibility at all.	Usually take inappropriate responsibility on themselves when they should be ensuring that others take it.	May not expect to be given responsibility and may at first fail—but, when trusted, prove to be highly responsible.

The challenges of leading as a child are specific to each of the four ego patterns. Each has a different set of issues, born out of their own particular 'childlike posture'. The table above outlines some of the specific responses Shapers, Definers, Adapters and Defenders will tend to make to the call to lead 'as a child'.

The invitation to lead as a child involves a specific response that will leave behind the comfortable and familiar way in which we inhabit the world. Undefended leadership turns on its head the world's conception of power and embraces the notion that we must become as little children in order to lead others. Being childlike is an essential component of leadership—I believe, because we are fundamentally, by our very nature, always children of God. If we fail to acknowledge this, our childlike needs become suppressed and channelled into unhealthy childish fantasies, destructive, unnamed and irresponsible. Mature childlikeness is a quality of playfulness, awareness and wonder, trust and taking responsibility that overturns society's conventional priorities. It replaces fear with confidence and offers others a courageous generosity.

Study questions 13

1. How would you have dealt with that bullying problem?
2. This chapter suggests that childlike leadership can be more efficient. Why, and how?
3. Do you agree?
4. Can you think of a similar situation you have encountered in your own role as a leader?
5. What are the chief characteristics of childlike leadership?
6. How do you react to Eleanor's story?
7. What does it make you want to go and do?
8. This chapter suggests that if we don't lead in a childlike way, it may result in childishness. How might this be manifested?

⊃ On the website, www.theleadershipcommunity.org, join in the online discussion on 'Leading like a child'. You need to be registered as a free 'guest member' in order to join the discussion.

9. How does this chapter challenge you to change
   · as a person?
   · as a leader?

FOURTEEN

The Formation of Moral Authority

We began this book by observing the lives of some of the world's most undefended leaders. The characteristic common to them all was what I called 'moral authority'—that quality in their lives, values and ideals that in itself gave them authority among their peers. What we also noticed was that another thing these leaders often shared was a history of struggle. If we are to know what it is to truly lead, we need to look more closely at the nature of struggle and how leaders respond to it.

Nature should alert us to the intrinsic good of struggle. If you see a butterfly struggling to escape from its chrysalis, you may be tempted to lend it a helping hand. Most of us don't like to see creatures struggle and it would seem a kind thing to do. However, you would be condemning it to an early death. The struggle the butterfly has to fight its way out is vital for strengthening its wing muscles. Nature builds in struggle as an essential part of the formation and development of healthy life.

It is, perhaps, a uniquely modern ideal that we should eliminate struggle through constant improvements in our socio-economic conditions. We have become increasingly defended against pain and loss, through technological advances and growing economic power. It hasn't been so for most of human history—and, indeed, it still isn't so for most of the global community to this day. It is the preserve of the global elite to contemplate a life from which struggle may be banished. But perhaps, like the emerging butterfly, we risk being fatally weakened if we embrace such a vision of ease. Could our defendedness against hardship render us more fragile as a result? Could there be a strength to those who, through choice, live lives undefended against distress? Could there be qualities of endurance, fortitude, courage, determination and patience that are formed only through such experiences? Again, as parents we often encourage our children not to give up, whether learning an instrument or practising their basketball skills. We seem to know that the effort they put in, however boring or hard, is worthwhile. And yet at the same time we take it as our prerogative as adults to avoid such 'labour' and 'pain' as far as possible.

Struggle takes many forms, and one man's effort is another man's ease. It may be physical: the father who labours to earn enough so his family can eat that night, or the mother who walks five miles with a child on her back to fetch water from a clean well, or the disabled person for whom simply cooking an ordinary meal is a huge task, or the child who walks eight miles to school every day because there isn't one in her village. I remember watching an elderly woman, crippled with rheumatoid arthritis, hobbling, inch by inch over five minutes, to make it up to the rail in church to take holy communion. It struck me that every action of my day, which I do without a second thought, would be for her a struggle, a battle of will against pain.

Struggle may be physical. It may also be emotional: the mother who has lost her daughter in a car accident, for whom each day begins and ends with the sickening emptiness and loneliness of that loss, or the sufferer from depression who fights to keep his head above the grey tide of pointlessness that threatens to overwhelm him, or the victim of rape trying desperately to control her rising panic when she finds herself alone in a room with a strange man, or the couple who have watched each of their tiny babies, born prematurely, die within a few hours from some unknown condition.

Struggle may be physical, it may be emotional. It may also be intellectual: the writer who defies a tide of critical opinion to find the courage and self-belief to express what he feels called to say, or the child, battling against a school system that has labelled him 'low-performing' in his first year, or the scientist, searching for a solution to the medical condition to which he has devoted the whole of his working life, or the chief executive endeavouring to lead his company through a major transition when the welfare of hundreds of employees depends on his choices, or the leader of a community whose beliefs are ridiculed and marginalized by the society in which they live.

Struggle may be physical, it may be emotional, it may be intellectual. And it may also be spiritual. Perhaps the great struggles all end up being spiritual in the sense that they pose us ultimate questions. Victor Frankl was a Jew incarcerated in the Nazi concentration camp at Auschwitz. As he looked around him, he saw his fellow inmates succumbing to the appalling conditions. What he noticed was often those who received news of the death of a loved one died soon after. It was as if they lost the will to live, lost the reason to endure the pain. Frankl resolved not to lose his sense of meaning and purpose himself. Everything else could be taken from him, but the Nazis could not take that. In the face of his suffering, his own personal meaning became the one thing that was secure.

Having survived the war, Frankl went on to develop a psychological tradition that places at its centre the need of each human being to find their own meaning. His ideas have been rather trivialized in the post-war boom as 'meaning' has become synonymous with little more than personal fulfilment; but for Frankl it was always far more than that. Meaning was not 'the icing on the cake' which you added once you had accumulated all the possessions you needed to be comfortable. Meaning was the irreducible core of our human being, which could never be taken away. For Frankl, meaning was found through the struggle for life, through the deprivation of virtually all other human needs.

His story alerts us to the essential role of suffering in the formation of leaders. Suffering in itself is not the 'good': we are not called to be masochists, seeking out painful situations as if there were some nobility in them. No, it is a stimulus that causes us to struggle, and in this struggle it is possible for certain qualities to be fashioned. However, it is also possible that the pain will prove overwhelming and, rather than forming our humanity, will have the effect of dehumanizing us. What makes the difference, it seems, is the choices the struggler makes: their response to their pain. It is this that determines whether the knife will shape or cripple, whether the fire will consume or refine.

When we are made to struggle, we are assailed by all kinds of emotions, emotions that can, at worst, harden into negative and destructive attitudes. The emotion of fear makes us instinctively defend ourselves, for example. What matters is how we then process our experience of it. Do we allow it to become anxiety, which may in turn express itself in depression or self-harm or other anxiety disorders as we try to 'hold' our feelings? Or do we allow the fear to turn into anger? Anger may turn into rage, and rage into hate; and hate may harden into suspicion, hostility and aggression and erupt into actual violence. Violence may in turn bring retribution, and thus you find yourself in a cycle of destruction chosen from the outset by your reaction to pain and struggle. It is all too easy for an experience of suffering to lead to a cycle of defendedness, territoriality and aggression.

Struggle offers us choices: it sets before us diverging paths, as it were, and obliges us to choose between them. This is its nature. Much of life allows us to drift along indecisively, not committing ourselves to one thing or another. Pain and struggle allow no such ambivalence. We are forced to choose, and often the path we take becomes one that determines our destiny. What choices, then, do those who we recognize as leaders with moral authority make when they are faced with pain in their own lives?

Purpose and purposelessness

The first choice is between purpose and purposelessness. When we are in pain, we ask the question: Why? Why us? Why now? In the face of such questions, the need to find a purpose to the experience, a meaning that makes it significant, is acute and pressing. Churchill's political career up to the age of 65 was chequered with failure. He had suffered for most of his life from depression, an experience so familiar he named it his 'black dog', like an old hound always lurking in the background. On his appointment as Prime Minister in 1940, he remarked that his whole life had been a preparation for this moment. He had been born with a sense of destiny, an expectation that one day he would be called to some great act. This sense of purpose drove him on through his depressions and mistakes. It made sense of his failures and prevented him from sinking into self-pity.

Two 20th-century poets, one American and one Welsh, express the contrasting choices that lie before us when we encounter pain. T S Eliot in 1942 wrote that

> *The one discharge from sin and error…*
> *Lies in the choice of pyre or pyre—*
> *To be redeemed from fire by fire.*[16]

For Eliot, the necessary, unavoidable route by which we are purged of self-attachment and fear was a painful one; to be defended against it would have been comfortable but ultimately self-defeating. By contrast, Dylan Thomas wrote possibly his best-known lines about the prospect of old age and death:

---

[16] T S Eliot, 'Little Gidding' from *The Four Quartets,* in *Collected Poems 1909–1962* (this edn Faber and Faber, 1963). Reprinted by permission of Faber and Faber Ltd, London and Harcourt, Inc., Florida

Do not go gentle into that good night,
Old age should burn and rave at close of day;
Rage, rage against the dying of the light.[17]

In the face of purposeless loss (in this case, the loss of youth and faculties), suffering and ultimately annihilation, rage and fury become valid options, which Thomas would encourage us to embrace. The stark difference between the two responses lies in the meaning of the suffering. For Eliot, it had significance in the formation of his ultimate identity. For Thomas, it was meaningless and in itself confirmed only the futility of human life. I want to suggest that the formation of the leader is to be found in Eliot's choice as opposed to Thomas's. This is not to be insensitive, I hope, to the trauma of pain or to insist that we stoically battle on with a stiff upper lip. Grief often accompanies pain and loss and we must support those who journey with that dark companion. However, slowly, over time, that journey may become more purposeful again. The person who chooses courageously to hold on to a belief in the purpose of their life and the value of their experience of pain will emerge refined, able to carry others through their own suffering. People find purpose through pain in different ways: a mother may find purpose in the loss of a child to illness by starting a campaign in their memory for better awareness of the condition and better funding for research. An athlete may find purpose in the loss of a limb in a car accident in the appreciation of mobility that it gives her and the way it inspires her to campaign for greater resources for disabled children to enjoy sport.

The journey through pain that the Shaper must make is, of course, different from the one that lies ahead of the Definer, or the Adapter, or the Defender. For the Shaper, pain may be something of which they have relatively little knowledge, and that which they have experienced they have buried. Their hunger for safety can lead them to deny their pain and seek relationships in which they will be insulated from it. For the Definer, the pain of failure, or of a broken relationship, can be the catalyst for monumental life-change. Often, they will perceive such moments as 'conversions' that turned their lives around. These can fill their lives with purpose and meaning, as they become evangelists for the new reality they have discovered. For Adapters, pain is the very stuff of life: they have learnt to live with it, to accommodate it. For them, the threat is to be defeated by it, whereas freedom involves believing in the greater purposes that can be achieved through it. Defenders are often motivated by pain, and their experiences of injustice, marginalization and exclusion can drive them to try to build a different and (one hopes) better world.

---

[17] Dylan Thomas, 'Do Not Go Gentle'. By Dylan Thomas, from THE POEMS OF DYLAN THOMAS, copyright ©1952 by Dylan Thomas. Reprinted by permission of New Directions Publishing Corp. and David Higham Associates

Love and anger

There are those who manage to make meaning out of their own pain and, in so doing, overcome the potential futility of their struggle and the rage and resentment that could have festered in their loss. However, this kind of passion can be fuelled as much by unresolved pain as by genuine freedom, and it is this that alerts us to the second choice that has to be made at the crossroads of pain: that between love and anger. The emotion of anger is powerful and it is not in itself wrong. However, for an activity to be inspired and driven by anger, let alone a mission, is dangerous. Ultimately, anger overturns and tears down. Anything energized by it will in the end prove destructive.

Emma had been damaged at birth through faulty medical procedures. The neurological consequences meant that she was significantly disabled, both physically and mentally. Her father struggled with anger at the negligence that had caused this, though he chose not to sue the hospital. His way of coping with his sadness was to see purpose in Emma's life as it was. He believed she was someone who would teach others about disability, acceptance, tolerance and humanity. This became a purpose in which he invested enormous and ever-growing energy. As he came up against systems that marginalized her and ignored her, as a child, a pupil or a member of the community, he fought them and refused to give in. Those around him, however, detected increasing rage in his zeal. Conversations with him continually turned back to the subject of injustice. His concern became blinkered as he saw everything in terms of the cause. Increasingly, he fell out with those who were trying to help, regarding them as lacking the necessary fight for the crusade he believed in so passionately. He reduced his friends to confused outsiders and become confrontational. In a way, he increasingly manifested the patterns of behaviour of the Defending Ego: seeing others as threats and seeking to protect the vulnerable from them. In the end, he seemed to have been robbed of his ability to trust.

Emma's father was tanked up as a social leader with a purpose; but his fuel was not love but anger, an unresolved resentment that leaked out and damaged others around him. There are many in social leadership like him. Sometimes, those who themselves have experienced life as unjust, those who have an embedded Defending pattern, become the most vociferous campaigners for social justice. However, their actions are fuelled not by love but by anger, and so they are not free. The pain we suffer forces us to struggle to find the resources to cope, and sometimes anger can seem to offer us a wellspring of motivation that could get us through it. The deeper struggle, however, is to find a source of power and energy drawn not from anger but from love.

Love seems so absent when we are suffering. Surely love would protect us from pain? Surely love would not allow us to struggle so? Once again, Eliot offers us his conclusion about the ultimate source of pain. He writes:

> *Who then devised the torment? Love.*
> *Love is the unfamiliar Name*
> *Behind the hands that wove*
> *The intolerable shirt of flame...*[18]

Can it be that Love allows us to suffer, to struggle? What kind of love is that? We may catch a glimpse of such love in the choice some parents make for their child, suffering from cancer, to undergo painful surgery and nauseating chemotherapy. In the face of illness for which the only cure is painful, love chooses that path. Could it be that, if as a human being each one of us is sickly, infected with the wrong kind of self-protection, the only cure available to us is one that involves pain and suffering? Could it be that, if we have taken refuge in a place we think is safe that is actually full of danger, it is through pain that Love calls us to escape? Not that we seek pain, of course; but when it finds us, we may choose to see it as a tool to be used in our formation.

In the place of struggle, where can we find the face of Love? We may find it in the tender hand of a loving partner who nurses us. We may find it in the patient ear of a friend who listens to us hour after hour. We may find it in the warm embrace of a child who presses their love into us. We may find it in the gentle breeze and warm sun on an afternoon's walk. We may find it in the letters and e-mails and flowers we receive from those concerned for our wellbeing. We may find it in the prayers of a faith community that upholds us in our hours of darkness. We may find it in mystery: simply in a deep knowledge that One loves us and we are not alone.

The unconditional regard, approval and affection that we all need to make us safe is most deeply needed when we are in pain—but often hardest to find. Accessing Love is not a one-off experience, not something that 'just happens to us' when we're not looking. We need to continue deliberately and in a disciplined way to put ourselves in the place of Love so that we can continue to draw on its strength.

For Shapers, experiencing and receiving this love for ourselves may not be difficult, but we have to take care that complacency and ill-discipline don't creep in. At the same time, we need to recognize that love is always received as a gift, to be generously given away. If instead we see it as a possession and hoard it, it quickly turns sour and rancid.

---

[18] T S Eliot, 'Little Gidding'

For Definers, receiving love is an alien experience: we are more at home doing something to earn it or justify it. We may find it helpful to look out for how often we clench a hand into a fist, or grip a bag or a briefcase like a vice—when we find ourselves doing so, it's time to smile and relax that grip that reveals our determination not to be robbed of what is ours. Instead, we should open our hands and allow them to receive, and then give away, the things that briefly come into our stewardship.

For Adapters, receiving love involves believing we are worthy of it. The trick is to make sure that we capture every single act of love, gesture of blessing and word of grace and affirmation. We could try keeping a little book in which we note down all these little instances and experiences—it is a great discipline, as long as we make sure that it's an expensive book, beautifully bound, not a scrappy, dog-eared old notebook!

For Defenders, the key is perhaps to let go of our anger. Anger can become bottled up inside us, a dangerous source of passion and drive. It needs to be released, like the pressure in a volcano that will produce a violent eruption if it finds no other escape. Then, we must take the risk of entrusting ourselves to others again. Even though it feels immensely risky, it is a risk worth taking so that our wounds can be gently healed.

Many leaders have found it essential to practise a spiritual discipline of prayer on a regular basis to sustain this. Gandhi was well known for adhering to his routine of praying and reading scripture in the early morning and resting in the afternoon, even if it meant that meetings with political leaders had to be delayed! Such a rigorous regime and rhythm, I suspect, gave him the steel to survive the enormous pressure—including hostility—he often faced. Today, a growing number of business leaders are planning-in regular retreats on which they can refresh their inner being. As one of the Bible's maxims puts it: 'Above all else, guard your heart, for it is the wellspring of life' (Proverbs 4.23).

Knowing who we are and knowing what we do

The choice between purpose and purposelessness, the choice between Love and anger. The third choice that struggle forces us to make is that between knowing who we are and knowing what we do. Leaders are often busy people; many are instinctive activists, bursting to take on any new challenge that presents itself. In such a life, it is all too easy for someone to know themselves only through the things they do, the roles they play. Indeed, their activism may be a strategy to distract them from the emptiness behind the amazing things they're achieving. Struggle changes all that. Often, it takes from us our ability to be busy, to be in control through our own managerial skill, our expertise and the systems we have put in place. When we're in pain, we're often incapacitated, taken out of the action and unable to influence it. From this position of enforced passivity and powerlessness, we have to confront a stark question: Who are we? The Definer will ask: Who am I, without the props of my job around me? The Adapter will ask: Who am I, without the feedback from my acolytes and underlings? Or without the affirmation of being essential to every board meeting, vital to the corporation, indispensable to everyone around? All four egos will ask: Who am I, when I am alone, when the mobile is silent and the in-box is empty and the world goes on without me? Who am I then?

In a place of struggle, we must find an answer that is not related to our activities or roles. We are challenged to find an identity that is not threatened by the loss of such things, that is deep enough and robust enough to survive when the props of our old lives are removed. The question becomes simply: Do I know who I am? At this point, when everything else has been taken away from us, this question is not an academic one—it is urgently practical. The solution is not to speculate philosophically on the nature of identity. Rather, it is to look for the enduring qualities and characteristics that have survived, and can survive even a devastating loss.

One of the most striking things about the Jewish religion is the centrality of memory and storytelling. The Jewish scriptures tell the story of the nation, from the call of the patriarch Abraham, back in Genesis 12, to the return of the people from exile in Babylon in the seventh century BC. The faith of the Jews involves retelling this story as well as enacting rituals that remind them of central events within it. Chief among these are the rescue and exodus of the people from Egypt, an event remembered in the festival of the Passover. The Jews find a sense of corporate identity in the story that is told of how God accompanied them through their history. In the face even of devastating loss—even of their homeland during their exile—they retained this sense by retelling the story of God being with them.

In a place of struggle, we are forced to choose: whether we see our pain as a pointless agony against which to rail or, as the Jews did, as a period of growth, possibly even of transformation, in which a deeper and bigger Presence accompanies us. Oppressed by loss—of our role, or our job, or our health, or a loved one—we are forced to come to know ourselves, not as people defined by such things but as people who choose not to be overcome. We might say we are invited to see ourselves as those who, like the Jewish people, have walked an accompanied journey, one on which we were not alone. And we are invited to regard this journey, like them, not as one that has no purpose but as one that has brought us to the meaningful place in which we now confidently stand. Once again, it is the presence of and our relationship with Another through our journey that enable us to endure. The man or woman who can look back on their life and see it as a series of accompanied events and transitions in which they 'found themselves' is the man or woman who can not only survive struggle but can face any threat without fear.

Many Shapers and Definers have coped with life's harsh challenges through denial, blocking out the pain and the memory of pain and pressing on. For them, there can be no freedom: they can't go back to their story for a knowledge of who they are because they have spent a lifetime erasing it from their remembrance. They have chosen the path of defendedness, and, faced with a new threat, they can survive only by continuing denial.

Many Definers have coped with failure in their past through domination. Seeking to prevent a recurrence of such experiences, they have amassed skills and competencies so that they are 'in control' of their circumstances, able to cope. They, too, have chosen the path of defendedness. Faced with a new threat, they can only hope they have the power to overcome it.

Many Adapters have coped with the pain in their past through fear and anxiety, allowing themselves to be pushed back into a corner, ruled—indeed, continually assaulted—by their memories of what was done to them. They, too, have chosen the path of defendedness. Faced with a new threat, they can survive only by cowering and hoping not to be overwhelmed.

Many Defenders have coped with their past struggles through anger, not allowing the wounds ever to be healed or forgotten, but instead letting them fester and infect everything they do. And they, too, have chosen the path of defendedness. Faced with a new threat, they can survive only by lashing out.

Denial, domination, defeat and anger over our past cannot help us to grow through suffering and struggle in the present. The only route to growth lies through owning our past and taking responsibility for it. More than that, it lies through finding meaning in it and recognizing that it has not been a solitary journey but one on which we have been accompanied, known, loved and understood. It is then we can begin to find meaning and healing in the story we have told, and the freedom to face the future. It is then that as leaders we find the freedom to 'lead out of who we are'.

We could say that the leader who has not reached this point is a leader who doesn't know whether they are anything more than their success. Indeed, if we are to become leaders who are able to embrace the prospect of our own personal demise for the sake of the choices we believe are right, then answering the question of our ultimate worth, beyond the roles we play, becomes not optional but imperative. Our great leaders all had the courage to offer their followers not an easy ride to ensure their own popularity, but struggle and hardship to achieve the greater goal. On 13 May 1940, in his first speech as Prime Minister, Winston Churchill said: 'I have nothing to offer but blood, toil, tears and sweat.' Not a great manifesto—but the embattled British responded to what they perceived as his total commitment. They may not have liked the message, but in the coming years a depth of admiration, affection and even, perhaps, dependence was forged between Churchill and the nation he led that has rarely been surpassed in a political leader. Undefended leaders are perhaps not often the most popular at the outset, but they are usually the most needed by the end.

None more so than Mahatma Gandhi. 'Rivers of blood may have to flow before we gain our freedom, but it must be our blood!' said the frail, birdlike man to his people. Yet people followed him because of his authenticity and trustworthiness. All the positional power of Lord Mountbatten, as well as the military power of his troops, could not shape the fate of India as that one man could. This kind of leadership does not offer easy promises or wide, open roads; rather, it recognizes and embraces a future of obstacles and opposition. Such leadership requires the leader to be in a place of personal security, where their own success, comfort, reputation and popularity do not impinge upon their purpose and direction, where they are genuinely free to 'lose' their personal status to achieve the greater goal of leading others to freedom. They are free because, ultimately, their identity does not depend upon their success; and they are followed because everyone else recognizes this to be the case. Their moral authority, forged in the flames, is clear for all to see.

Study questions 14

1. Do you agree with the assertion of this chapter that struggle is 'a good thing'?
2. In what ways have you personally grown through struggle?
3. Do you ever regret avoiding struggle that might have been beneficial?
4. What are the three choices that struggle sets before us?
5. Which poet, T S Eliot or Dylan Thomas, inspires you more in this regard? Why?
6. How can you begin to draw from a well of love rather than anger?
7. What changes to your routine or regime may you need to make to ensure that this happens?
8. Are there parts of your life where you live in denial, in defeat or in anger?

⊃ On the website, www.theleadershipcommunity.org, listen to the audio file with the 'visual landscaping' exercise 'Remembering the journey of your formation'. This important exercise will help you to become more aware of your own accompanied journey and to understand it as meaningful and known. You need to be registered as a free 'guest member' in order to listen to the audio file.

FIFTEEN

Setting Undefended Goals

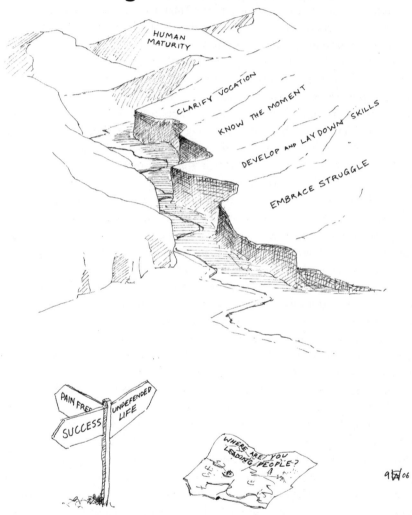

Virtually every book on leadership you read emphasizes the importance of setting goals and having clear, achievable objectives. The value of being clear, purposeful and deliberate in your choices is without doubt; the value in helping others to become clear, purposeful and deliberate in their choices is also without doubt. However, what is less clear is what those choices should be in favour of. The mere fact that someone can identify clear targets does not make them a good leader. There was no doubt that Adolf Eichmann was a highly efficient goal-setter: he determined to execute the 'final solution of the Jewish question' (the extermination of the Jews in Europe) hammered out at the now infamous Wannsee Conference outside Berlin on 20 January 1942. History tells of the horrible efficiency with which he and the Nazi machine he mobilized put it into effect. Setting goals and achieving targets are of no value in themselves unless the goal we have in mind is the right one.

What, then, is the right goal of leadership? Of course, there is, in an obvious sense, a different goal in every situation: to get the children safely across the road, to prepare the product for launch, to take the country through a war or the company through a 'downsizing', to captain the team to win a tournament and so on. However, beneath these specific goals, is there a deeper goal to leadership? Is there a greater task that unifies the act of leading?

One answer to that might be that the goal of leadership is success. The leader always leads her followers towards success, whether that is making it across the road or winning the tournament or the war. Many people define the goal of leadership as success: they point out that the alternative is to be happy with failure. No leader wants to lead people to that. Consider how much leadership you experience is aimed towards the goal of succeeding. What is the goal in business? Better sales, stronger forecasts, shorter turnaround. How about in education? Better Sats results, better degree results. How about in life in general? A better salary, a nicer house, a smarter car, more exotic holidays, a better healthcare policy, a better pension. Life, as a whole, is oriented around success, and leadership at almost all levels takes this as the unquestioned target. To succeed is good; to fail is bad. Good leaders aim for success. Good leaders achieve a better rate of success than bad leaders.

But I am not so sure. For a start, success in itself is not always a good thing. It may come at a price—an unreasonable price, be it financial or moral or personal. I can get my children to succeed in their homework. I can do it for them, or help them to search for answers on the Internet. I can get them extra tuition. I could probably ensure that they get good grades in all their coursework throughout school if I chose. That would be success of a kind—academic success. Maybe they would get to go to a fine university if so. That, too, would be success in one sense. But in another sense my strategy might have been very unsuccessful. It would probably have failed to enable them to grow up: to learn themselves, take responsibility, have integrity and deal with failure.

I can lead my family towards a better lifestyle—move to a smarter area, drive them around in a bigger car, take them on nicer holidays—but at the end of the day I could find myself cursed by children who never saw me because I was working such long hours. I can push my children to find 'suitable' spouses of such a standard (in other words, good enough in my eyes) that they will never be happy in their relationships. I can leave a wife who is unable to explore and develop her own gifts because I need her to be around to maintain the domestic ecology. Leadership in life, if measured in terms purely of 'success' (if these are understood as they usually are), does not necessarily equate with good leadership at all. Conversely, undeniable examples of good leadership often fail by the criterion of 'success', at least in the short term. The situation in India got worse, not better, following independence. Mother Teresa never persuaded the world to change its trade policies, never secured significant sums of aid to transform Calcutta. Aung San Suu Kyi remains under house arrest in Myanmar, where the brutal military dictatorship has only tightened its grip on power. And there have been occasions when quite exceptional leaders have lost their lives—surely the ultimate sign of personal defeat—as martyrs for their cause.

This should alert us to the fact that the general goal of success in leadership that we may set ourselves is mistaken. I want to suggest that the only proper goal of leadership is this: to enable people to take responsibility. My belief is that leadership is concerned with the task of helping people to move towards fully mature, responsible personhood. 'A responsible person'—a term that slips off the tongue, almost a cliché. Yet so much of our lives often involves the rejection of responsibility. Some of us live in deceit, concealing things about ourselves and our habits. Some of us live in blame, charging other people with things for which we should be taking responsibility. Some of us live in hypocrisy, expecting other people to live up to standards we would never dream of attempting. Some of us live in denial, choosing to forget about things we have done or had done to us for ill. Taking appropriate responsibility is more difficult than it seems—we have spent much of this book examining the mechanisms in all of us that often cause us to take either too much or too little. My suggestion is that enabling people to take responsibility is the primary task of leadership. It is not part of the task. It is not something we hope will occur as a spin-off. It is the explicit target at which we aim. Everything else is secondary.

My suggestion is that the goal towards which we lead our followers is in fact a human goal: it is for both the leader and the followers to be changed. This, after all, is the only thing that both the leader and the followers have in their power to change. It's not in our power to create success. It's not in our power to make other people do things. It's not in our power to dictate the course of world events (though we may believe it is). We cannot predict, let alone dictate, whether the stock market will go up or down, whether our team will win the league or not. But what we can take responsibility for is ourselves, and those we are responsible for leading. That is our sphere of influence. It is (to put it in spiritual terms) God's job to raise up rulers, and to bring them down again. What folly to think we have the power of success and failure! What conceit to think it is our gift to decide who lives and who dies! We do not have the power of life and death—those keys belong to Another.

Our task, as human beings, as human leaders, is far more humble and close to home. It is to grow up. It is to learn, through the experiences we are given, who we are—what it means to be courageous, what it is to serve, what it is to be loved and to love, what it is to be real, what it is to be fully human. True leadership is leadership of ourselves and others into this kind of life: embracing our full humanity, discovering what it is to be fully human, to participate fully in the world. Once we understand this, we begin to understand that leadership is not restricted to the narrow range of activities it is often supposed to be. It is not simply 'motivation'; it is not simply 'inspiring others to great efforts', nor is it simply courage. Leadership is not simply executive decision-making or being clear about strategy and how to achieve your goals. Leadership is the activity—any activity—that leads other people more deeply into this full humanity: which enables them to take hold of, and take responsibility for, the life that they, as a unique, particular person within the created human race, have been given to live.

Leadership, therefore, is a task that occurs at every level of life and in every kind of sphere—at the swimming pool, in the nursery, around the dinner table, in the car, on the phone, in the classroom, in front of the television, in the garden. Leadership is a way of offering life to the world, in order to draw life out of the world. As such, it is a spiritual activity.

What, then, are the goals we should set for ourselves if we are to develop into significant leaders? There are, of course, skills we need to develop: skills such as communicating, listening, thinking, planning, enabling, negotiating, persuading and so on. Leaders should set themselves goals to develop such skills, and we will be addressing how to do this in the second book of this trilogy. However, there are some more fundamental goals for which we must aim, which take priority over the developing of any skills.

Enabling people to embrace struggle

We may need to put a health warning on leadership for the benefit of those who seek to avoid pain, or want others to avoid it: Leadership is not for you! Leadership is fatally undermined by two flaws in the leader. The first is when she cannot allow either her work or those she leads to fail. Most of the time, the people we lead don't want to take responsibility for their actions—they would rather we did it. As long as the leader comes along after them, mops up their mistakes, patches the whole project back together, prevents the show coming off the rails, their followers will allow them to do so. The show may go on, but the followers themselves are not being led. They're being protected and pampered.

Sometimes a leader can behave like a footballer trying to win the game single-handed, who runs everything himself instead of passing the ball to someone else. Even if such a leader succeeds, she will not have helped the team to improve. What she usually does succeed in doing is running herself ragged, getting frustrated and probably angry at everyone else. I see team after team whose leader in effect carries the 'children'. They are quite happy to be carried, and they never have to stand on their own two feet. Most people (including us) only take responsibility when things start actually to go wrong. Then, the pain motivates us to do something about it. If the leader can't stay with the pain and face failure herself, how will the followers ever manage to? All the undefended leader has to focus on is making the pass—getting the ball into the right zone. If the other player doesn't get to it, this is an issue the whole team has to deal with, not just the leader. Being undefended in this way is immensely liberating: rather than feeling under pressure to succeed all the time, the undefended leader is free to take risks, to delegate, try new challenges and, above all, be honest. Moreover, when things go wrong, she can avoid blaming others (when it's their responsibility) or herself (when it's not). Get the ball into the right zone—that's all she has to do.

The second fatal flaw in a leader is offering premature solutions. All too often, I see business leaders, frantic to get improvements in their company's performance, come up with new idea after new idea, and none of them last. Why is that? Because they are premature solutions. A solution will only work when its time has come. And that time is when people are crying out for it, desperate for something to change. The role of the leader is often, in fact, to make the situation worse so that it can get better. He needs to be the one who can allow things to go wrong and let people struggle and fail—for only then will people start to take responsibility for the situation and the choices they make. A leader who is a Mr Fixit is no leader at all. The basic role of the leader is to 'push the problem back to the followers'—push it back under their noses, so they can't try to deny it and bury it. It is to make sure that the truth of the situation remains visible, rather than hiding it away. Then people start to experience being trusted; they start to learn and begin to trust themselves. In this regard, undefended leading is rather like being a skilled teacher: you could tell your students all the answers, but you don't. You hold back, allowing them to work them out for themselves. Your role is to help them apply themselves to the problem, trust themselves and find the resources to solve it.

Enabling people to both develop and 'lay down' their skills

The concept of the leader as someone who makes it possible for the gifts of others to emerge is well established. She doesn't seek to be the most competent person on her staff; she doesn't seek, or need, to be the expert. Instead, she seeks to gather around herself capable, skilled people who she can then develop further. She releases the gifts in others, through her trust, her support, her encouragement and inspiration. The cliché that a leader should 'do herself out of a job' is true.

However, what is less widely understood is the role of the leader in enabling people to 'lay down' their skills. This is, perhaps, much harder than developing and releasing the skills of others. The possession of a skill is not in itself necessarily a gift to the community or organization. We have seen how our skills are, in fact, assets we use to acquire the approval, power and control we need to make ourselves secure in the world. As long as they are used in this way, they can't set other people free. That is not to say that your skills cannot be used to train and help others—of course they can. That's what you might call 'low-level leadership', in which skills are imparted. What I mean, however, is that for higher levels of leadership, in which the leader's task is less practical and more emotional, social and spiritual, the leader's own freedom from the need to use her skills to acquire anything is paramount. The power we possess and the skills we have cultivated are of no use in higher-level leadership until they have been laid down, let go. The leader is called to relinquish control over what binds her, and what she binds to herself, in order to be truly free. Only then can she set others free. She herself is called to let go of what she owns. This is the journey a leader must make, to the quiet, still, sanctified place of self-offering where she is available to be used. All the mystical writers acknowledge this journey. The great leaders such as Jesus, Gandhi and King speak of their knowledge and acceptance of this place: the place where they have let go and laid down their own power to make change happen.

The goal of the leader, therefore, must be not only to develop skills in others but to enable others to be willing to lay down their skills. Often this involves the leader inviting people periodically to step down from their leadership roles in order to renew their experience of freedom. I myself believe that all leaders should lay down their roles every five years or so. A period in which we are shorn of our power is good for us and reveals whether we are truly free. This is more than a sabbatical. It should be undertaken on an understanding that that role and that power may not necessarily be taken up again. They should be genuinely let go and handed over. This also ensures that a leader experiences once more what it is like to be led, and to receive before she gives.

Many good leaders cannot get to this place: it is too painful, it asks too much of them. Their skills remain their own personal possessions. As such, they remain skills—they cannot become 'gifts'. A gift is something we give away to others, for their benefit, not our own. This means—tragically—that they will always exercise their leadership with a desire to preserve themselves. Of course, this is a place where all of us, not only leaders, need to go to be set free. But this is a book about leadership, and it's worth pointing out that most leaders have more to give up than most other people. They are probably leaders by virtue of their skills: their power and training and personality. They lead because people accept their influence. For them, then, it is harder to let go. They have more to lose. However, what they will discover when they do let go is that what they have let go is given back to them once more.

Self-emptying leads to transformation; it leads to empowerment. In my own experience, I have found that many of the skills I have possessed that I have also let go have been given back to me, but with a power they did not have before. My intellectual skills were given back to me, but not in the field I thought best—medicine, for which I was highly unsuited—but in theology, in which I have found the greatest and deepest challenge I could have imagined. My skills as an athlete were given back to me. The very year I let them go, after three years of underperforming on the track, I set new college records, beyond all my expectations. And I am finding now that the professional work I gave up as lost, and handed over, has been given back to me—except that it is new, different and (I sense) better. Giving things up is always painful, but once the battle is over, there is a great sense of freedom, of lightness.

Enabling people to identify and embrace their vocations

It is the central proposition of this book that life observes a fundamental principle. When someone is willing and able to give away what they possess, they find that it is given back to them transformed into something greater. This is the argument I have been developing, from different angles, from the first page. The leaders who leave the finest legacies in history are those who participate in this transaction. Leaders who fail to do so will always be limited in their power and their ability to create lasting freedom through their influence. I believe it is through this act of consecration that a leader becomes aware of what may properly be called his 'vocation'. Vocation, from the Latin *voco*, means simply a calling. It doesn't refer only to a religious calling. Rather, a sense of vocation is available to each of us. Vocation is that clarity of identity and purpose, power and freedom, that you gain when you are truly available. Vocation occurs when the gifts and opportunities you were willing to 'lay on the altar' are given back to you, now shining bright, transformed by some other Power and Presence.

If I am right in this, then the task of leading is no longer primarily a complex business of theories and ideas and training schemes (though all of these things could undoubtedly enhance your work). Instead, it is fundamentally this: the single focus of the consecrated man or woman who has laid aside their personal interest and made their whole being, their skills and their resources, available to be used for the good of others. At this point, I believe, they find themself playing in harmony with the universe, taking part in a drama much bigger than themselves. This means that potent leadership—undefended leadership—can be offered by the simplest person to the most qualified. Intelligence, wealth, status become irrelevant. The only relevant factor is the degree of consecration, of availability.

Thus, a leader enables others to identify and embrace their own vocations. This is not career guidance. This is more than identifying some passion or drive or skill that might suit a particular job or role. This is helping someone else to come to understand what their unique and specific calling in the world may involve. Of course, vocation emerges slowly and continues to deepen over time, and it needs testing from many different sources. No single leader should presume to tell another person what their vocation is with absolute certainty. But this question should be in the back of every higher-level leader's mind: What sense of vocation do I find emerging in the person in front of me? I often look out for people with exceptional listening skills—the ability to sit quietly without interrupting or interpreting, to notice little things and to reserve judgement. These, rather than the confidence of power, are the things I would look for in a potential leader.

Enabling people to 'know the moment'

There is a distinction in classical Greek between two kinds of time. *Chronos* means 'time' as in minutes, hours or years, but *kairos* means a significant time— a season, a moment, an occasion. It is not unreasonable to say that Western civilization have been built largely on an appreciation of *chronos* but with very little appreciation of *kairos*. As a Westerner, I am brought up to worry about how long things take, whether things are late or not, how much time I have wasted. Western industry is based on the principle of efficiency: achieving the maximum output in the least amount of time. We often appoint and 'incentivize' men and women as our 'leaders' on the basis of their skill and with a mandate to 'make the system more efficient'. In fact, this virtually defines the role of the CEO in any corporation—to reduce costs and increase productivity. And for this they are handsomely remunerated.

Our system rewards those who have skills in managing *chronos* better than others. However, as leaders our goal is to develop in our followers a growing confidence in their *kairos*. Higher-level leadership involves helping people to understand the times in which they live. In part, this is a matter of appreciating the historical, social, political and spiritual context we find ourselves in. It is about helping people to learn how to see under the surface, to read between the lines, to discern the larger patterns and bigger forces at work. It is about helping people to notice things that would otherwise pass them by, to teach them to be good 'seers' whose eyes are always open. It is about helping people to discriminate between truth and lies and to pursue the truth with all their heart. It is about fostering the poet, the artist and the prophet in our followers: those who see beyond the veil that is drawn over our eyes. Leaders need to allow such diverse skills to flourish—which is why any healthy society encourages and funds the arts and allows freedom of speech. We should be cautious of leadership that sacrifices depth on the altar of efficiency.

Our society greatly undervalues those who have the ability to recognize *kairos*, yet we do so at our peril. We live in a day when mere increases in productivity are not going to solve the world's problems. Whatever our governments may tell us, the answer to global warming does not lie in more efficient technology. At current rates, it would require two Earths to allow the present population of the world the levels of consumption Britain now enjoys, and five Earths to allow them all American levels of consumption! There simply is not enough planet to solve our problems through increasing our efficiency and reducing our waste. The only answer is going to be cutting our consumption.

I find myself looking for leaders who already choose to live according to such principles. Whether or not they can afford more, I am impressed by the person who has chosen to limit their spending to moderate levels and invest their income in the greater things they believe in. It tells me that they are free from the need to acquire more. In an age when all of us have to become more acutely aware of how we are consuming the Earth's resources, this is the kind of person I want leading me.

This, then, is our *kairos*, the time we find ourselves in. Of course, the *chronos* system is resisting this conclusion for all it is worth, insisting that the world is not going to change, that time (*chronos*) will march on as it always has, insisting that rumours of crisis (*kairos*) are exaggerated. Indeed, we do need to beware those leaders whose claim to status rests on their predictions of apocalypse.

But recognizing the significance of the time we live in does not mean we must become apocalyptic. Often, this is just another way of abdicating responsibility. Rather, we must recognize that today (as on all days) we are called to have moral courage, to pursue an undefended life, to resist the forces in and around us that lead people into defended places. That moral choice begins in simple ways with our lifestyle and ends, simply, in our own enjoyment of undefended freedom. The happy coincidence is that as we ourselves enjoy this undefended life, so others, too, begin to be led into freedom.

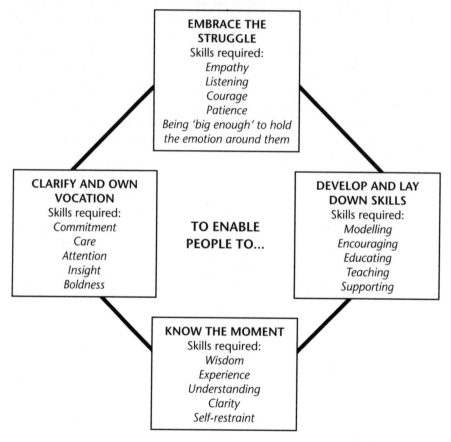

Diagram 15.1   The goals of the undefended leader

Study questions 15

1. What, in your opinion, are the strengths and weaknesses of a *chronos* leader and a *kairos* leader?
   - *chronos*
   - *kairos*

⮑ On the website, www.theleadershipcommunity.org, join in the online discussion '*Chronos* or *kairos*?' You need to be registered as a guest member in order to join the discussion.

2. What is the most lasting thought this book will leave you with?
3. Imagine being able to stand and watch your own funeral. What would you want those who give tributes to say about you, as a person and as a leader?
4. What are the greatest obstacles standing in the way of you being the person or leader you'd like to hear described?
5. What support do you need now to help you?
   - a peer mentoring group?
   - training on leadership strategies?
   - reflection on and development of your own character?
   - a community of fellow leaders facing similar challenges to you?

⮑ We may be able to help you with some of these. The website www.theleadershipcommunity.org has many useful links to further training and resources. There may be fees payable for these further resources.

Reading List

R F Baumeister, L Smart and J M Boden. 'Relation of Threatened Egotism to Violence and Aggression: the Dark Side of High Self-Esteem', *Psychological Review* 103

John Bowlby. *Attachment and Loss*. New York: Basic Books, 3 vols, 1969–80

Clayton Carson, ed. *The Autobiography of Martin Luther King*. Abacus, 2000

T S Eliot. 'Little Gidding' from *The Four Quartets*, in *Collected Poems 1909–1962*. Faber and Faber, 1963

Robert Fulghum. *All I Really Need to Know I Learned in Kindergarten: Uncommon Thoughts on Common Things*. New York: Ballantine Books, 2003

Robert M Galford and Anne Seibold Drapeau. *The Trusted Leader*. The Free Press, 2002

Manfred Kets de Vries. *The Leadership Mystique: A User's Manual for the Human Enterprise*. Financial Times Prentice Hall, 2001

James Lawrence. *Growing Leaders: Reflections on Leadership, Life and Jesus*. Bible Reading Fellowship, 2004

Joseph LeDoux. *The Emotional Brain*. London: Phoenix, 1999

Jae Yun Moon and Lee Sproull. 'Essence of Distributed Work: The Case of the Linux Kernel'. *First Monday* 5, No. 11 (November 2000)

Larry C Spears, ed. *Reflections on Leadership: How Robert K. Greenleaf's Theory of Servant-Leadership Influenced Today's Top Management Thinkers*. John Wiley & Sons, 1995

Margot Sunderland and Nicky Armstrong. *Helping Children who Bottle Up their Feelings & A Nifflenoo Called Nevermind*. Speechmarks, 2004

Dylan Thomas. 'Do Not Go Gentle' in *Collected Poems 1934–1953*, edited by Walford Davies and Ralph Maud. Phoenix, 2000. Reprinted by permission of New Directions Publishing Corp., NY, and David Higham Associates, London

Jim Wallis. *Faith Works: Lessons on Spirituality and Social Action*. SPCK, 2002

Afterword: The Leadership Community and The Undefended Leader Profiling Tool

The Leadership Community

In reading this book, you have in effect joined a growing community of leaders who are seeking to explore undefended leadership. The Leadership Community is an international network of people involved in leadership in business, charity, politics or the church. It provides many resources for those who want to offer undefended leadership, including training and other courses, conferences, web tools and, of course, access to each other's wisdom.

At www.theleadershipcommunity.org you can register for free as a *guest member* of The Leadership Community in order to access the online activities that support this book. There are also additional fee-paying resources available on the website as well as information about conferences and training courses.

The Leadership Community is committed to practice: we are members because we are trying to *live out* a certain kind of life. The only condition of membership is that you choose to join us.

The Undefended Leader profiling tool

If you are in leadership, you may benefit from profiling your own ego. We have developed a unique, web-based psychometric tool, The Undefended Leader Profile™, that can do this quickly and accurately and gives you helpful feedback. It will develop the general observations about ego patterns in this book into a specific diagnostic of your own particular patterns.

The Undefended Leader Profile™ has been devised by Simon Walker and uniquely analyses:

> your front- and backstage strategy—which stage you concentrate on, how you use both stages and what impact your strategy may have on others;

The Undefended Leader Profile™ is a derivative of the Personal Ecology Profile™, which was developed by Simon Walker at Oxford University in 2002. The Personal Ecology Profile is a proprietary tool of Human Ecology and has won several awards in Britain.

- your ego pattern—which ego pattern(s) you follow, Shaping, Defining, Adapting or Defending.

The Undefended Leader Profile™ will:
- present your results in the form of a clear, single-page score chart;
- generate a simple representation, in the form of diagrams, of your front- and backstage strategy and your ego pattern;
- provide a lucid and concise account of how these will shape your behaviour, your emotional life and your needs;
- show you the important differences between your strategy and the strategies others may use;
- provide helpful guidance on how you can achieve greater undefendedness in your life and leadership;
- link you directly to the right exercises and resources in The Leadership Community that are particularly suited to support your growth in undefended leadership.

Click on www.theleadershipcommunity.org/profile for more information about the benefits and costs of The Undefended Leader Profile™, and to use it.

Forthcoming in
The Undefended Leader trilogy
by Simon Walker

**LEADING WITH
NOTHING TO LOSE**

Training in the Exercise of Power

ISBN-13: 978 1903689 448

**LEADING WITH
EVERYTHING TO GIVE**

*Disarming the Powers and
Authorities*

ISBN-13: 978 1 903689 455

*"Leadership is commonly associated with dominance and
power. Simon Walker shows that there are other types of
leadership capable of being more effective."*

R Meredith Belbin*

*Peter Berger,
The Sacred
Canopy.*

editions

www.piquanteditions.com

*R Meredith Belbin, a previous chairman of the Industrial Training Research Unit and founder
member of Belbin Associates, is the author of several management titles, including *The Coming
Shape of Organization* (1996).